Cool Story Programs

for the School-Age Crowd

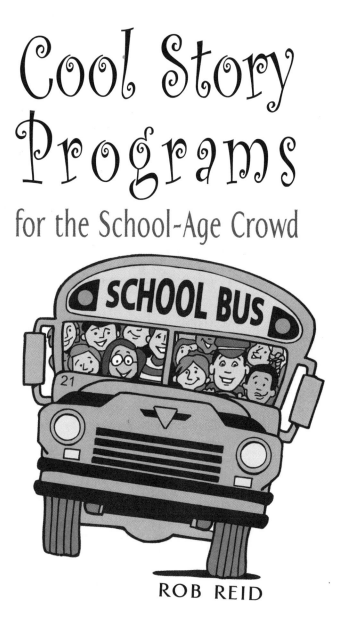

ROB REID

American Library Association
Chicago 2004

Composition by ALA Editions in Aperto and Berkeley using QuarkXPress 5.0 on a PC platform

Printed on 50-pound white offset, a pH-neutral stock, and bound in 10-point coated cover stock by McNaughton & Gunn

The paper used in this publication meets the minimum requirements of American National Standard for Information Sciences—Permanence of Paper for Printed Library Materials, ANSI Z39.48-1992. ∞

Library of Congress Cataloging-in-Publication Data

Reid, Rob.
    Cool story programs for the school-age crowd / Rob Reid.
      p. cm.
    Includes bibliographical references and index.
    ISBN 0-8389-0887-X (alk. paper)
    1. Children—Books and reading. 2. Children's literature—Study and teaching (Elementary)—Activity programs. 3. Reading (Elementary)—Activity programs. I. Title.
Z1037.A1R45 2004
028.5′5—dc22   2004009933

Printed in the United States of America.

08 07 06 05 04   5 4 3 2 1

Dedicated to all students and staff
who walked through the halls of
Boyd Elementary School in Eau Claire, Wisconsin

CONTENTS

INTRODUCTION

You won't find story program themes about teddy bears, bunny rabbits, or choo-choo trains in this book.

What you will find is an exciting, offbeat mix of story program themes ranging from "A-1 Stories" to "Catching Some Zzzzzz's" and a cool assortment in between: underwear and stinky stuff, rats and their cousins, teachers and principals (both the good and the mean), aliens and frogs, and a host of bad guys and gals found throughout the history of children's literature, from monsters and witches to the legendary Big Bad Wolf.

This resource was designed to inspire public children's librarians, school media staff, and classroom teachers to make literature come alive for elementary-school-age children, with particular focus on kids in kindergarten through fourth grade (with a little tweaking to get those fifth and sixth graders involved).

The amount of materials and resources available for this target audience is greater than what one can find for preschoolers. For the elementary-school-age crowd, teachers and librarians will find a wealth of writing activities, reader's theater and creative dramatics, musical activities, poetry activities and choral readings, short stories, and selections from chapter books to replace those fingerplays and felt-board stories.

Story Programs for the School-Age Crowd

Many public libraries offer traditional story programs for preschoolers but not for those kids who have started elementary school. Public library programs for this age tend to be special events, such as theme parties like a Harry Potter or Captain Underpants party. The intent of the programs in this book is to encourage public libraries to continue offering story programs on a regular basis for elementary-school-age children. These programs can be offered on a weekly or monthly basis during an evening, weekend, or after school. If this type of schedule proves to be too taxing on library staff, the programs in this book can still be designed for special events offered during special times, such as Children's Book Week.

Advertise these programs by the various theme titles, such as "What Stinks?" or under a fun series title, such as "Cool Stories for the School-Age Crowd." Avoid simply calling them "Story Programs" because of the association of those words with the younger traditional preschool story programs. In fact, discourage parents from bringing preschoolers to these programs. The elementary-school-age children appreciate having their own events.

Schools have the advantage of already having a captive audience for the programs found in this book. It is hoped that both media specialists and classroom teachers will find a lot of fun ideas here to use with their students.

How to Use This Book

Each chapter includes a "Lesson Plan at a Glance," a thumbnail sketch of the entire program for quick reference. Each program theme includes a variety of picture books, chapter book selections or short stories, poetry and wordplay, and some type of activity, such as creative dramatics, reader's theater, writing, music, sports, or crafts.

Each theme is different in the type and number of formats used, depending on what is available on the market. There are plenty of picture books and poems that fit each theme, even the more offbeat themes. Some themes, such as the "Big and Bad" series, rely heavily on folklore, while other themes, such as the "School" series, depend on chapter books and activities to round out a solid program. Although many resources go out of print at an alarming rate, a conscious effort was made to include only books and recordings that were readily available for purchase at the time this book was written.

The "Preparation and Presentation" section provides detailed suggestions for using these various resources. Story program leaders are encouraged to adapt the lesson plans to fit their particular styles and strengths. With that in mind, each chapter has "Mix and Match" sections of supplemental materials to suit a variety of moods and preferences.

I'm a great believer in adapting the same program for different audiences. Thus, the "Tweaking the Program Theme" section gives suggestions on taking the program that you've used with the elementary-school-age crowd and, with some minor age-appropriate adjustments, using the same program for slightly younger children (preschoolers) or slightly older kids (fifth and sixth graders).

Finally, the "And Yet Even More Titles for You to Consider" section contains out-of-print books that may still be found in library collections, time-tested favorites that have been covered extensively in other story program resource guides, or books that I haven't personally used but have heard from others who have used them with great success.

The Different Components of a Lesson Plan

Picture Books

Many picture books are better suited for elementary-school-age children than preschoolers. Although many kindergarteners and first graders still enjoy the same picture books they enjoyed as preschoolers, they, and slightly older students, are also ready to appreciate a new level of picture book. Many picture books are set in elementary schools and speak directly to this target audience. There are several rich folklore picture books by authors such as Eric Kimmel and Demi. And, of course, folktale parodies by authors such as Jon Scieszka and Margie Palatini are perfect for school-age children. With the wide range of sophisticated picture books on the market today, virtually no one is too old to appreciate a good picture book.

Poetry

My intent in using poetry with this age group is to "sprinkle" poems throughout each program. Many poems are natural tie-ins to books and other resources. Many poems can be enjoyed alone on their own merits. Several poems lend themselves to choral readings that involve the audience. Others can be used for writing activities that aren't confined to classrooms.

Chapter Books and Short Stories

Chapter book selections, whether an entire chapter or short passages are read, have been included to encourage the kids to read the rest of the book. Many selections end with a cliff-hanger. However, there is nothing wrong if children don't wish to pursue the rest of the story and simply enjoy the passage for its entertainment value. Many of the short stories scattered throughout the programs are self-contained forms of entertainment. Once in a while, a child will check out the collection that contains the short story, either to enjoy the story all over again or to investigate companion stories. Some of the chapter book selections and short stories are fairly lengthy for a library story program. Story program leaders are encouraged to practice reading the passages aloud ahead of time and to edit for time constraints, if necessary.

Oral Tales

Oral tales are designed to entertain the audience through the art of story-telling—no books or scripts present. The story program leader takes the time to learn and practice the story and retell it in his, or her, own words. Of course, those program leaders who aren't comfortable with the storytelling process can still share the same stories by reading them aloud. For those novice storytellers interested in learning more about techniques, I highly recommend the following books:

> Bauer, Caroline Feller. *Caroline Feller Bauer's New Handbook for Storytellers.* ALA, 1993.
>
> Livo, Norma J., and Sandra Rietz. *Storytelling: Process and Practice.* Libraries Unlimited, 1986.
>
> MacDonald, Margaret Read. *Twenty Tellable Tales.* Wilson, 1986.

Reader's Theater

Reader's theater activities are great fun for elementary-school-age children. Those audience members who can read can entertain the nonreaders with a "cold" or unrehearsed performance from scripts provided by the story program leader. There are several reader's theater scripts available both as book collections and online; select titles are noted throughout this book.

Original reader's theater scripts are fairly easy to create. Find an enjoyable story in print form that is heavy on dialogue and light on descriptive passages. Easy reader books and picture book editions of folktales are particularly strong sources. Simply use the author's exact dialogue and place it in your adaptation. Assign the descriptive narrative passages to two or more readers to make the script flow in a lively manner. As long as your performance is used for classroom or noncommercial library story program use, you do not need to apply for permission to adapt the script.

Ask for volunteers from the audience to read the various roles. Let them know that they shouldn't worry about giving a polished, error-free reading since they haven't had time to rehearse. The readers enjoy this type of participation. There's no need to memorize lines or blocking. They get to perform while holding on to their "security blanket," or script. Encourage them to simply let the power of the words entertain the audience. They do not need to cross over and engage the other readers as if they were in a play. The readers simply stand or sit on a bare stage area with little or no costumes and props. Tell them to imagine that they are speaking into a floor microphone and that if they move away from the mike, the audience will not be able to hear them.

The kids in the audience love this type of entertainment. Reader's theater is more akin to storytelling and reading aloud than conventional theater in that the audience members get to visualize the characters and settings in their imagination.

For more help in developing reader's theater activities, I highly recommend visiting Aaron Shepard's wonderful reader's theater web site at www.aaronshep.com/rt.

A Final Word on the Offbeat Themes Found in This Book

I get bored easily. Sometimes this boredom leads to programming burnout from using the same materials and themes over and over again. What excites me about leading a story program is locating new material and using new and old favorites in an exciting new way—mostly by developing an unusual lesson plan theme.

Instead of selecting a theme first and then trying to find materials to use with that theme, I usually pick one or two core books or stories and look for a connection between the two. That connection, no matter how thin it may be between the two books, becomes the theme. I then add other material that may contain even thinner connections. The key is to add strong material to a program, not mediocre material just because it fits a theme.

For example, I found myself wanting to share both Lisa Wheeler's picture book *Old Cricket* and *Click, Clack, Moo: Cows That Type* by Doreen Cronin. Normally, I would have used the first book with an insect theme and the latter title with a farm theme. This time, however, I noticed the alliterative connection between the two titles. I searched for other stories, poems, and activities that had examples of alliteration and assonance. Thus, "Clickety-Clackity, Creaky-Squeaky Stories" became a fun story program. Not only was this theme different from the norm, but it was an easy, lively way to promote the program in signage, flyers, news releases, and classroom visits. It was an incredible amount of fun locating the material and then assembling it into a lesson plan—much more rewarding than hauling out the same old "Food" story program theme for the umpteenth time.

Try this approach to create new story program lesson plans yourself. In the meantime, enjoy these eighteen *Cool Story Programs for the School-Age Crowd.*

ONE

A-1 Stories

Lesson Plan at a Glance

MUSICAL ACTIVITY:	"One Finger, One Thumb"
PICTURE BOOK:	*One Grain of Rice* by Demi
POEMS:	Selections from *A Burst of Firsts: Doers, Shakers, and Record-Breakers* by J. Patrick Lewis
READER'S THEATER:	*Anansi and the Magic Stick* by Eric Kimmel
PICTURE BOOK SELECTION:	"Grasshopper Logic" from *Squids Will Be Squids* by Jon Scieszka
POEM:	"Alligator Pie" from *Alligator Pie* by Dennis Lee; and *The Twentieth Century Children's Poetry Treasury*, edited by Jack Prelutsky
WRITING ACTIVITY:	Creating New Verses for "Alligator Pie"
PICTURE BOOK SELECTION:	"Little Walrus" from *Squids Will Be Squids* by Jon Scieszka
PICTURE BOOK:	*Aunt Flossie's Hats (and Crab Cakes Later)* by Elizabeth Fitzgerald Howard
CRAFT ACTIVITY:	Creating a Memory Hat (for Aunt Flossie)

Preparation and Presentation

The theme implies that these are top-notch, star-quality stories and activities. I selected titles that either begin with the letter *A* or else feature the number 1. This allows for a lot of flexibility and doesn't confine one to select materials for a narrow theme. The possibilities are nearly endless. You can also carry out this concept for the other letters of the alphabet and numbers. (See the chapter 3 theme, "Three.")

MUSICAL ACTIVITY

"One Finger, One Thumb." Anonymous

You can follow the music on one of the recordings listed below or simply chant the words and wait for the giggles. Feel free to make up your own verses or solicit ideas from the kids. Here is the version I use:

1. One finger, one thumb, keep moving,
   (Wiggle one finger and one thumb.)
   One finger, one thumb, keep moving,
   One finger, one thumb, keep moving,
   And we'll all be happy today.

2. One finger, one thumb, one elbow . . .
   (Keep adding the new moving body parts.)

3. One finger, one thumb, one elbow, one head . . .

4. One finger, one thumb, one elbow, one head, one tongue . . .

5. One finger, one thumb, one elbow, one head, one tongue, two feet . . .

6. One finger, one thumb, one elbow, one head, one tongue, two feet, stand up/sit down . . .
   And we'll all be TIRED today.

The tune to this popular, traditional, action song can be found on the following recordings:

Allard, Peter, and Ellen Allard. *Sing It! Say It! Stamp It! Sway It! Volume 1.* 80-Z Music, 1996. Ordering information can be found at www.peterandellen.com; 1-888-SING-IT-1.

Wee Sing Children's Songs and Fingerplays. Price Stern Sloan, 1988.

PICTURE BOOK

Demi. *One Grain of Rice.* Scholastic, 1997.

> A clever girl outwits a selfish raja in this tale from India. The mathematical concepts introduced in this book are ideal for the elementary-school-age crowd. The foldout pages will entrance kids, especially the illustration of the 256 elephants carrying 536,870,912 grains of rice. This is one of the best-designed picture books of all time.

POEMS

Lewis, J. Patrick. *A Burst of Firsts: Doers, Shakers, and Record-Breakers.* Illustrated by Brian Ajhar. Dial, 2001.

> Celebrate notable firsts such as "First Men on the Moon," "First Person to Go over Niagara Falls in a Barrel—and Survive," and "#1 Lunch Choice of School Kids."

READER'S THEATER

Kimmel, Eric. *Anansi and the Magic Stick.* Illustrated by Janet Stevens. Holiday House, 2001.

> Anansi discovers that Hyena has a magic stick that does all of the work. Anansi steals the stick, but things quickly get out of hand. This is a fun story to use as a reader's theater script. There are parts for nine readers: Anansi, Warthog, Lion, Zebra, Hyena, and four narrators. Simply take Kimmel's text and type out the dialogue. Divide the narration like the following example:
>
> > Narrator 1: It was a fine bright day. All the animals were
> > Narrator 2: working
> > Narrator 3: working
> > Narrator 4: working
> > Narrator 1: in their gardens. All except Anansi the Spider. Anansi lay in his front yard, fast asleep. Warthog, Lion, and Zebra came walking by.
>
> Half the fun of creating reader's theater is in developing the script. Trust me.

PICTURE BOOK SELECTION

Scieszka, Jon. "Grasshopper Logic." In *Squids Will Be Squids.* Illustrated by Lane Smith. Viking, 1998.

> Share this short, derivative version of an "A for Aesop" fable about a grasshopper that surprises his mother with an incredible homework assignment.

POEM

Lee, Dennis. "Alligator Pie." In *Alligator Pie*. Illustrated by Frank Newfeld. Houghton Mifflin, 1974; and *The Twentieth Century Children's Poetry Treasury*. Edited by Jack Prelutsky. Illustrated by Meilo So. Knopf, 1999.

Read Lee's modern classic, nonsensical poem about Alligator Pie, Alligator Soup, and Alligator Stew.

WRITING ACTIVITY

Creating New Verses for "Alligator Pie"

Lead the audience in a group-brainstorming project for a new type of alligator food. Write the following pattern for all to see:

> Alligator _____, Alligator _____,
> If I don't get some, _____.
> Give away my _____,
> Give away my _____,
> But don't give away my Alligator _____.

Ask the audience to name a food item. Work with them to try to find words that rhyme with that item. The word that fits the third line does not need to rhyme with the words at the end of the other lines, but it should be a word somehow associated with the word that ends the fourth line. Here are two examples that kids have created in my programs:

> Alligator Bubblegum, Alligator Bubblegum,
> If I don't get some, gee, I'm gonna look dumb.
> Give away my trombone,
> Give away my drum,
> But don't give away my Alligator Bubblegum.

> Alligator Spaghetti, Alligator Spaghetti,
> If I don't get some, I think I'll throw confetti.
> Give away my Barbie doll,
> Give away my teddy,
> But don't give away my Alligator Spaghetti.

PICTURE BOOK SELECTION

Scieszka, Jon. "Little Walrus." In *Squids Will Be Squids*. Illustrated by Lane Smith. Viking, 1998.

Little Walrus reveals something embarrassing about the mother walrus. It's hard for me to read this short story aloud without stopping to laugh.

PICTURE BOOK

Howard, Elizabeth Fitzgerald. *Aunt Flossie's Hats (and Crab Cakes Later)*. Illustrated by James Ransome. Clarion, 1991.

Great-great-aunt Flossie shares her "boxes and boxes and boxes of HATS!" and tells the stories and memories behind each one.

CRAFT ACTIVITY

Creating a Memory Hat (for Aunt Flossie)

There are several simple hat craft projects on the Internet these days. Just type in the words *Crafts* and *Hats* in any online search engine, and you will find many easy, inexpensive projects for making hats. You can do this for any of the themes in this book. Have the kids make one of those hats after reading *Aunt Flossie's Hats (and Crab Cakes Later)* so that they'll be able to always have good memories of their library story programs.

Mix and Match Picture Books

Johnson, Angela. *One of Three*. Illustrated by David Soman. Orchard, 1991.

The youngest of three sisters describes their relationship. Some days are fun, but on other days she feels left out. Her parents do a nice job to make sure she becomes "one of three" with them.

Johnson, Stephen. *Alphabet City*. Viking, 1995.

This book features realistic paintings of urban landscapes and structures that resemble the letters of the alphabet. After looking at the pictures in the book, lead the kids around the library or school to look for letter-shaped objects throughout the building. Take pictures of those shapes with a digital camera, print the pictures, and create your own book titled *Alphabet Library* or *Alphabet School*. Thanks go out to one of my former students from the University of Wisconsin–Eau Claire for sharing this idea with me.

Lester, Mike. *A Is for Salad*. Putnam, 2000.

"A is for Salad?" That doesn't make sense until you show the kids a picture of an alligator eating a salad. Another example is "B is for Viking." The kids

see a picture of a beaver wearing a Viking hat. The book ends with "Z is for
. . . The End," and we see a picture of a zebra's derriere. Brainstorm with the
kids to develop their own crazy alphabet book in this creative style.

Wong, Janet S. *Apple Pie Fourth of July.* Illustrated by Margaret Chodo-Irvine.
Harcourt, 2002.

A Chinese American girl is embarrassed that her parents are cooking
Chinese food on the Fourth of July. "Americans do not eat Chinese food on
the Fourth of July," she complains. She finds later that, yes, they do.

Mix and Match Chapter Book Selections

Carroll, Lewis. *Alice's Adventures in Wonderland.* (Any edition.)

Here's a wonderful opportunity to share this classic. Read chapter 7, "A Mad
Tea Party," featuring the memorable March Hare, Mad Hatter, Dormouse,
and a multitude of frustrating nonsense.

Colfer, Eoin. *Artemus Fowl.* Hyperion, 2001.

Read the first chapter of the first book in the series featuring a twelve-year-
old criminal mastermind and his large, adult companion, Butler, who is
armed with a "Sig Sauer in his shoulder holster, two shrike-throwing knives
in his boots, a derringer two-shot up his sleeve, garrote wire in his watch,
and three stun grenades." This sentence alone will hook adventure fans.

Danziger, Paula. *Amber Brown Wants Extra Credit.* Putnam, 1996.

Start with the very short chapter 1. Amber lovingly gives her mother some
"Amberino" gift certificates. Amber will gladly perform a chore for each certificate. Go right into chapter 2. Amber claims that she's held captive by a
madwoman—her mother. Mom's mad because Amber's teacher sent home a
note, and Amber's room is a mess. Much to Amber's dismay, Mom is already
cashing in an "Amberino" certificate.

Roy, Ron. *The Absent Author (A to Z Mysteries).* Random House, 1997.

The first of an alphabetical series features Dink, Josh, and Ruth Rose. They
are trying to solve the mysterious disappearance of mystery writer Wallis
Wallace. Read chapter 3. Dink's belief that Wallace was kidnapped seems to
be confirmed by a mysterious note.

Mix and Match Music

Colleen and Uncle Squaty. "1-2-3 Four-Ever Friends." In *1-2-3 Four-Ever Friends* (recording). North Side Music, 1995.

McCutcheon, John. "All God's Critters." In *Howjadoo* (recording). Rounder, 1987.

Pease, Tom. "Love Grows One by One." In *I'm Gonna Reach* (recording). Tomorrow River Music, 1989.

Peter, Paul, and Mary. "Garden Song (Inch by Inch)." In *Around the Campfire* (recording). Warner Brothers, 1998.

Raffi. "Aikendrum." In *Singable Songs for the Very Young* (recording). Rounder, 1976.

Mix and Match Poetry

Adoff, Arnold. "Aaron." In *The Kingfisher Book of Family Poems*. Edited by Belinda Hollyer. Illustrated by Holly Swain. Kingfisher, 2003.

Brooks, Walter. "Ants, Although Admirable, Are Awfully Aggravating." In *The Random House Book of Poetry for Children*. Edited by Jack Prelutsky. Illustrated by Arnold Lobel. Random House, 1983.

Comora, Madeleine. "Ant Farm." In *A Pet for Me*. Edited by Lee Bennett Hopkins. Illustrated by Jane Manning. HarperCollins, 2003.

Florian, Douglas. "The Aardvarks." In *Mammalabilia*. Harcourt, 2000.

———. "Apple Picking," "Autumn Questions," and "Awe-Tumn." In *Autumnblings*. Harcourt, 2003.

———. "Aunteater." In *Laugh-eteria*. Harcourt, 1999.

———. "One Potato Chip." In *Bing Bang Boing*. Harcourt, 1994.

Hoberman, Mary Ann. "Anteater" and "Applesauce." In *The Llama Who Had No Pajama*. Illustrated by Betty Fraser. Harcourt, 1998.

McDermott, Gerald. "Anansi the Spider." In *Eric Carle's Dragons, Dragons*. Edited and illustrated by Eric Carle. Philomel, 1991.

Prelutsky, Jack. "An Auk in Flight." In *Beauty of the Beast: Poems from the Animal Kingdom*. Edited by Jack Prelutsky. Illustrated by Meilo So. Knopf, 1997; and in *Something Big Has Been Here*. Illustrated by James Stevenson. Greenwillow, 1990.

Proimos, James. "Poor Sammy Kaye." In *If I Were in Charge the Rules Would Be Different*. Scholastic, 2002.

Schertle, Alice. "Anteater." In *Hoofbeats, Claws, and Rippled Fins: Creature Poems*. Edited by Lee Bennett Hopkins. Illustrated by Stephen Alcorn. HarperCollins, 2002.

Sierra, Judy. "Antarctica Anthem." In *Antarctic Antics: A Book of Penguin Poems*. Illustrated by Jose Aruego and Ariane Dewey. Harcourt, 1998.

Silverstein, Shel. "Alphabalance." In *Falling Up*. HarperCollins, 1996.

Wise, William. "Allosaurus Makes Her Apology." In *Dinosaurs Forever*. Illustrated by Lynn Munsinger. Dial, 2000.

Tweaking the Program Theme . . .

. . . *For Preschoolers*

Drop Demi's picture book, the reader's theater presentation, and the two selections from Scieszka's book, and substitute the following picture books:

Fleming, Denise. *Alphabet Under Construction*. Holt, 2002.

> A mouse tries to build the alphabet through various aspects of construction, such as airbrushing the *A,* carving the *C,* pruning the *P,* and so on until he zips the *Z.*

Kaye, Buddy, et al. *A You're Adorable*. Illustrated by Martha Alexander. Candlewick, 1994.

> You can talk or sing this picture book version of the 1940's hit or show the pictures while playing the song from one of the following modern-day children's recordings:

> > The Chenille Sisters. *Teaching Hippopotami to Fly*. Can-Too Records, 1996.

> > Lithgow, John. *Singin' in the Bathtub*. Sony, 1999.

> > Sharon, Lois, and Bram. *Great Big Hits*. A&M, 1992.

Root, Phyllis. *One Duck Stuck*. Illustrated by Jane Chapman. Candlewick, 1998.

> A duck gets stuck in the mud and needs a legion of woodland critters to pull him out.

Keep the poem "Alligator Pie," but drop the writing exercise. Instead, add this finger play, "The Alligator and the Monkeys."

Five little monkeys swinging from a tree (*Hold up five fingers.*)

Teasing Mr. Alligator (*Put thumbs in ears and wiggle fingers.*)

"You can't catch me!"

Along comes Mr. Alligator (*Place palms together and make a "swimming" motion.*)

Quiet as can be and (*Say in a near whisper.*)

SNAP! (*Clap hands together.*)

Four little monkeys swinging from a tree . . . (*Repeat down to "No little monkeys swinging in a tree."*)

. . . For Fifth and Sixth Graders

Drop Howard's picture book and the follow-up craft activity, and substitute an oral telling of one of the following tales:

Climo, Shirley. *Atalanta's Race.* Illustrated by Alexander Koshkin. Clarion, 1995.

In this retelling of the Greek myth "Atalanta and the Golden Apples," the young protagonist declares that anyone who wants to marry her must beat her in a footrace.

Seeger, Pete. *Abiyoyo.* Illustrated by Michael Hays. Macmillan, 1986.

A musical boy and his magician father help save the town from the giant Abiyoyo.

And Yet Even More A-1 Titles for You to Consider

Barber, Barbara E. *Allie's Basketball Dream.* Illustrated by Darry Ligasan. Lee and Low, 1996.

Casanova, Mary. *One-Dog Canoe.* Illustrated by Ard Hoyt. Farrar, Straus and Giroux, 2003.

Compton, Joanne. *Ashpet: An Appalachian Tale.* Illustrated by Kenn Compton. Holiday House, 1994.

Dr. Seuss. *One Fish, Two Fish, Red Fish, Blue Fish.* Random House, 1960.

Goble, Paul. *Adopted by the Eagles.* Bradbury, 1994.

Hoberman, Mary Ann. *One of Each*. Illustrated by Marjorie Priceman. Little, Brown, 1997.

Hoffman, Mary. *Amazing Grace*. Illustrated by Caroline Binch. Dial, 1991.

Keller, Laurie. *Arnie the Doughnut*. Holt, 2003.

Koller, Jackie French. *One Monkey Too Many*. Illustrated by Lynn Munsinger. Harcourt, 1999.

Munsch, Robert. *Alligator Baby*. Illustrated by Michael Martchenko. Scholastic, 1997.

Pinkwater, Daniel. *Aunt Lulu*. Macmillan, 1988.

Polacco, Patricia. *Aunt Chip and the Great Triple Creek Dam Affair.* Philomel, 1996.

Radunsky, Vladimir. *One: A Nice Story about an Awful Braggart*. Viking, 2003.

Sierra, Judy. *Antarctic Antics: A Book of Penguin Poems*. Illustrated by Jose Aruego and Ariane Dewey. Harcourt, 1998.

West, Colin. *One Day in the Jungle*. Candlewick, 1995.

TWO

Clickety-Clackety, Creaky-Squeaky Stories

Lesson Plan at a Glance

Preparation and Presentation

Have a pitcher of water handy as you lead the audience through the most tongue-twisting, alliterative story program ever devised! Begin with my patented "Storyteller Warm-Ups."

OPENING ACTIVITY

"Storyteller Warm-Ups"

> Have audience members stand and stretch their mouths in exaggerated motions while going through the vowels. Next, have them pinch their cheeks and shake them. Have them gnash their teeth, and then lead them in "Tongue Push-Ups." Have them stick their tongues out and yell "One! Two! One! Two!" as they move their tongues up and down. They can also move their tongues sideways and in "loop-dee-loops" before sitting back down for the fun.

PICTURE BOOK

Wheeler, Lisa. *Old Cricket.* Illustrated by Ponder Goembel. Atheneum, 2003.

> A cranky, crotchety, cantankerous cricket fakes a "creak-creak-creak" in his knee to get out of work. He later adds a "crick-crick-crick" to his neck, a "crack-crack-crack" to his back, and a "hic-hic-hic" to his head. The kids will enjoy repeating the sentence, "You don't get to be an old cricket by being a dumb bug." His plan is thwarted by Old Crow: "You don't get to be an old crow by being a birdbrain."

POEM

Fleischman, Paul. "House Crickets." In *Joyful Noise: Poems for Two Voices.* Illustrated by Eric Beddows. HarperCollins, 1988.

> This poem from the Newbery Award–winning book is a natural follow-up to Wheeler's picture book. It discusses the advantages house crickets have over outdoor crickets. Ask a good reader from the audience or another staff member to read one of the cricket voices with you. The two narratives intertwine with plenty of chances to say "crick-et" simultaneously.

PICTURE BOOK

Cronin, Doreen. *Click, Clack, Moo: Cows That Type.* Illustrated by Betsy Lewin. Simon and Schuster, 2000.

> This book is one of the biggest hits of the new century. The cows discover an old typewriter in the barn and make new demands of the farmer. They

go on strike, and a duck acts as the go-between messenger. Have an actual old typewriter in the program area for kids to try out afterward. They'll get a kick out of the clickety-clack noises it makes compared to modern computer keyboards.

POEM

Pape, Donna Lugg. "The Click Clacker Machine." In *The Twentieth Century Children's Poetry Treasury*. Edited by Jack Prelutsky. Illustrated by Meilo So. Knopf, 1999.

This tongue-twisting poem has a lot of clicking and clacking sounds.

MUSICAL ACTIVITY

"The 'Clickety' Mary Had a Little Lamb." Adapted by Rob Reid.

Most kids are familiar with this nursery tune. Have them "sing" the song by clicking their tongues inside their mouth. Start out slow the first time around and then repeat it at a faster rate. The whole program area will be full of "click" and "clack" mouth sounds.

PICTURE BOOK

Edwards, Pamela Duncan. *The Worrywarts*. Illustrated by Henry Cole. HarperCollins, 1999.

We now move from the hard "click" and "clack" noises and into a wealth of W words. Wombat, Weasel, and Woodchuck make plans to wander the world. They grow concerned about wasps, water, wolves, weather, whirlwinds, warthogs, and other W-related worries. They prepare watercress-on-whole-wheat-bread sandwiches, waffles with whipped cream, walnut wafers, and, well, you get the idea. This is another wonderful wead, uh, read.

POEM

"Weather." Anonymous

Since the characters in Duncan's book worry about the weather, read this challenging old chestnut.

> Whether the weather be fine
> Or whether the weather be not,
> Whether the weather be cold

Or whether the weather be hot,
We'll weather the weather
Whatever the weather,
Whether we like it or not.

I once recited this poem at an intergenerational program. As soon as I finished, a little voice chimed up, "Whatever!" The whole place cracked up.

SHORT STORY SELECTION

Kipling, Rudyard. "The Elephant's Child." In *Just So Stories*. Illustrated by Barry Moser. Morrow, 1996.

Is there a more beautifully written story that begs to be read aloud? This treat to all storytellers is available in many picture book editions and anthologies. Don't edit a single word of Kipling's original classic, which sounds more like a folktale than many true folktales. The main character asks what the crocodile has for dinner. Through his adventure, we learn why elephants have trunks. Some of the tongue-tripping words and phrases include "the great grey-green, greasy Limpopo River, all set about with fever trees," "promiscuous parts," "permanently vitiate," "cool schloopy-sloshy mud-cap," "rash and inexperienced traveler," "the Kolokolo Bird," "the Bi-Coloured-Python-Rock-Snake," and, of course, the young protagonist's "'satiable curiosities."

PICTURE BOOK

McCall, Francis, and Patricia Keeler. *A Huge Hog Is a Big Pig: A Rhyming Word Game*. Greenwillow, 2002.

You can use this picture book with the audience as an activity. Have them guess the answers to the wordplay pattern. For example, when you say, "A puppy kiss," they have to guess two rhyming words that mean the same thing. In this case, the answer is "A pooch smooch." Show them a few examples and answers from the book, and then let them guess the rest. Some are easy, while some are slightly trickier. Most will elicit giggles. If they get stuck, give them the animal and they'll usually come up with the rhyme. Other examples are "silly rabbit/funny bunny," "cattle food/cow chow," "swamp croaker/bog frog," and "grandmother goat/granny nanny." The book ends with the nonanimal "happy father/glad dad."

ACTIVITY

Tongue-Twister Tests

Write several tongue twisters on slips of paper ahead of time. Place them in a container, and let each member of the audience draw one. Give audience members a few moments to read their tongue twisters and practice saying them aloud. Allow any willing participants to share their tongue twisters with the entire group. Match readers with nonreaders so that the younger children can participate. Many will want to draw more slips of paper. (There are times when I feel this activity could be the entire program. I speak from experience.)

Here are a few good sources for tongue twisters:

> Dr. Seuss. *Oh, Say Can You Say?* Random House, 1979.
>
> Rosenbloom, Joseph. *Giggle Fit: Tricky Tongue-Twisters.* Sterling, 2001.
>
> ———. *World's Toughest Tongue-Twisters.* Illustrated by Dennis Kendrick. Sterling, 1986.
>
> Rosenbloom, Joseph, and Mike Artell. *Giggle Fit: Tricky Tongue-Twisters.* Sterling, 2002.
>
> ———. *The Little Giant Book of Tongue-Twisters.* Sterling, 1999.
>
> Schwartz, Alvin. *Busy Buzzing Bumblebees and Other Tongue Twisters.* Rev. ed. Illustrated by Paul Meisel. HarperCollins, 1992.
>
> Tait, Chris. *Ridiculous Tongue-Twisters.* Illustrated by Buck Jones. Sterling, 2003.

Along with the above tongue-twisting books, include some of the poems from the "Mix and Match Poetry" section.

Mix and Match Picture Books

Atwood, Margaret. *Princess Prunella and the Purple Peanut.* Illustrated by Maryann Kovalski. Workman, 1995.

A purple peanut grows on the nose of the pompous Princess Prunella in one of the most fun and challenging reads since Dr. Seuss. Audience members will listen open-mouthed from the beginning line: "Princess Prunella lived in a pink palace with her pinheaded parents, Princess Patty and Prince Peter, her three plump pussycats Patience, Prue and Pringle, and her puppydog Pug."

Clements, Andrew. *Double Trouble in Walla Walla*. Millbrook, 1997.

Lulu's infectious way of funny talk spreads to her teacher Mrs. Bell, the school principal, and the school nurse. As Mrs. Bell tries to explain, "Lulu's been trying to razzle-dazzle me with some kind of lippity-loppity jibber-jabber." The entire text reads like this. The story makes a fun reader's theater adaptation.

Edwards, Pamela Duncan. *Some Smug Slug*. Illustrated by Henry Cole. HarperCollins, 1996.

A slug goes "strolling on soil" one summer day and encounters a slope, a salamander, a sparrow, a spider, a swallowtail, a skink, a squirrel, a stinkbug, a skunk, and other sibilant obstacles before finally becoming a "succulent slug." Edwards has written several alliterative picture books. Check them out both in the "Lesson Plan" above and the list at the end of the chapter.

Rylant, Cynthia. *Mr. Putter and Tabby Pick the Pears*. Illustrated by Arthur Howard. Harcourt, 1995.

Mr. Putter tries to climb the ladder to pick the pears from the tree, "but this year he had cranky legs. Cranky legs, cranky knees, cranky feet." Even Tabby the cat knows what getting old is like. She has a cranky tail that refuses to swish some days. Mr. Putter comes up with an ingenious scheme to pick the pears that utilizes underwear and a slingshot.

Spence, Rob, and Amy Spence. *Clickety Clack*. Illustrated by Margaret Spengler. Viking, 1999.

A little black train heads down the track with cars full of yaks, a troupe of ducks going quack-quack, tumbling acrobats, a red caboose in the back, and more. After each verse, have the audience chime in with "clickety clack, clickety clack."

Thomson, Pat. *The Squeaky, Creaky Bed*. Illustrated by Niki Daly. Doubleday, 2003.

This fun retelling of a traditional tale comes complete with a grandpa who wears pajamas covered with ying-yang symbols. A parrot provides comic relief. There are lots of opportunities for making sound effects and funny voices.

Wheeler, Lisa. *Sixteen Cows*. Illustrated by Kurt Cyrus. Harcourt, 2002.

Cowboy Gene hollers for his eight cows: "Mudskipper! Sissy Nell! Sassafras! Mazie Bell! Twinkle Toes! Honeydew! Buttercup! Suzy Q!" Cowgirl Sue calls for her eight cows: "Sunflower! Baby Face! Button Eyes! Charlotte

Grace! Jelly Roll! Peekaboo! Cinderbox! Bobbie Lou!" The trouble begins when the sixteen cows get mixed together. The audience will enjoy yelling the word "Moo!" throughout the story.

Wilson, Karma. *A Frog in the Bog.* Illustrated by Joan Rankin. Margaret K. McElderry, 2003.

A frog on the log in the middle of the bog grows bigger and bigger as he flicks one tick, sees two fleas, spies three flies, glugs four slugs, inhales five snails, and then encounters a big old gator.

Mix and Match Chapter Book Selections

One advantage of an open-ended theme such as "Clickety-Clackety, Creaky-Squeaky Stories" is that you can include virtually any chapter book that has an alliterative title.

Check out the following selections and then peruse the long list below for more potential reading selections.

Coville, Bruce. *The Monsters of Morley Manor.* Harcourt, 2001.

This book features monkeys, monsters, and the weirdest house in Owls' Roost, Nebraska. After Old Man Morley dies, plans are made to sell off the manor's possessions before it's torn down. Read chapter 2, "Monkey Business." While at the estate sale, the protagonist purchases a box with the words "Martin Morley's Little Monsters." Upon investigation, he sees little monster figurines named Gaspar, Albert, Ludvilla, Melisande, and Bob. The chapter ends with the fingers of one of the figurines beginning to move.

Cox, Judy. *Mean, Mean Maureen Green.* Holiday House, 2000.

Lilley Nelson is worried about learning to ride a bike, the frightening neighborhood dog, and Maureen Green, the school bully. Rumors about Maureen have her giving one girl a "swirly" (ask the kids what that means if you don't know) and sticking another kid in a garbage can. Read part of chapter 4, "The Great Cookie Caper." Lilley's friend Adam concocts a cream cookie filled with toothpaste. Begin with the sentence "I have a great idea" and read to the end of the chapter. Read the first part of chapter 5, "Bruno." Maureen bites into the cookie. End with the line "You're dead meat, Lilley Nelson!"

Curtis, Christopher Paul. *Bud, Not Buddy.* Delacorte, 1999.

Bud, an orphan in 1936, goes on a search for the man he believes is his father. Before he does that, however, he must escape his foster home and the mean boy Todd, who sticks a pencil up Bud's nose. When Bud defends himself, Todd's parents stick Bud in a shed. Read chapter 2, which ends with the line "The padlock snapped shut with the loudest click I'd ever heard."

Here are more chapter books that contain alliterative titles (which is the only excuse you need to include them in this program) for your consideration:

> Atwater, Richard, and Florence Atwater. *Mr. Popper's Penguins*. Little, Brown, 1938.
>
> Fleming, Ian. *Chitty Chitty Bang Bang*. Random House, 1964.
>
> Giff, Patricia Reilly. *Poopsie Pomerantz, Pick Up Your Feet*. Delacorte, 1989.
>
> ———. *Tootsie Tanner, Why Don't You Talk?* Delacorte, 1987.
>
> Gilson, Jamie. *Double Dog Dare*. Lothrop, Lee and Shepard, 1988.
>
> Howe, James. *Dew Drop Dead*. Atheneum, 1990.
>
> Lowry, Lois. *Gooney Bird Greene*. Houghton Mifflin, 2002.
>
> Mahy, Margaret. *Tingleberries, Tuckertubs, and Telephones*. Viking, 1996.
>
> Myers, Walter Dean. *Me, Mop, and the Moondance Kid*. Delacorte, 1988.
>
> Pilkey, Dav. *Captain Underpants and the Perilous Plot of Professor Poopypants*. Scholastic, 2000.
>
> ———. *Captain Underpants and the Wrath of the Wicked Wedgie Woman*. Scholastic, 2001.
>
> Thomas, Jane Resh. *The Princess in the Pigpen*. Clarion, 1989.
>
> Van Draanen, Wendelin. *Sammy Keyes and the Search for Snake Eyes*. Knopf, 2002.
>
> Van Leeuwen, Jean. *Hannah's Helping Hands*. Phyllis Fogelman, 1999.

Mix and Match Poetry

Anonymous. "Betty Botter," "I Thought a Thought," and "Ned Nolt." In *A Bad Case of the Giggles*. Edited by Bruce Lansky. Illustrated by Stephen Carpenter. Meadowbrook, 1994.

Bishop, Morris. "Song of the Pop-Bottlers." In *Knock at a Star: A Child's Introduction to Poetry*. Rev. ed. Edited by X. J. Kennedy and Dorothy M. Kennedy. Illustrated by Karen Lee Baker. Little, Brown, 1999.

Ciardi, John. "Frizzing." In *The Twentieth Century Children's Poetry Treasury*. Edited by Jack Prelutsky. Illustrated by Meilo So. Knopf, 1999.

Dr. Seuss. "Quack, Quack!" In *Read Aloud Rhymes for the Very Young*. Edited by Jack Prelutsky. Illustrated by Marc Brown. Knopf, 1986.

Florian, Douglas. "Double Dutch Girls" and "Fireflies." In *Summersaults*. Greenwillow, 2002.

———. "If Your Car Goes." In *Bing Bang Boing*. Harcourt, 1994.

Greenfield, Eloise. "Grandma's Bones." In *The Kingfisher Book of Family Poems*. Edited by Belinda Hollyer. Illustrated by Holly Swain. Kingfisher, 2003.

Hoberman, Mary Ann. "Permutations." In *The Llama Who Had No Pajama*. Illustrated by Betty Fraser. Harcourt, 1998.

———. "Yellow Butter Purple Jelly Red Jam Black Bread." In *Yellow Butter Purple Jelly Red Jam Black Bread*. Illustrated by Chaya Bernstein. Viking, 1981.

Kumin, Maxine. "Sneeze." In *The Twentieth Century Children's Poetry Treasury*. Edited by Jack Prelutsky. Illustrated by Meilo So. Knopf, 1999.

McCord, David. "The Pickety Fence." In *Knock at a Star: A Child's Introduction to Poetry*. Rev. ed. Edited by X. J. Kennedy and Dorothy M. Kennedy. Illustrated by Karen Lee Baker. Little, Brown, 1999.

Miller, Calvin. "Alphabet Protest." In *A Bad Case of the Giggles*. Edited by Bruce Lansky. Illustrated by Stephen Carpenter. Meadowbrook, 1994.

Nash, Ogden. "The Sniffle." In *The Twentieth Century Children's Poetry Treasury*. Edited by Jack Prelutsky. Illustrated by Meilo So. Knopf, 1999.

Prelutsky, Jack. "Yak." In *Eric Carle's Animals, Animals*. Edited and illustrated by Eric Carle. Philomel, 1989; and in *The Random House Book of Poetry for Children*. Edited by Jack Prelutsky. Illustrated by Arnold Lobel. Random House, 1983.

Unobagha, Uzo. "Clicking, Clicking, Round My Ankles." In *Off to the Sweet Shores of Africa and Other Talking Drum Rhymes*. Illustrated by Julia Cairns. Chronical, 2000.

Tweaking the Program Theme . . .

. . . *For Preschoolers*

Drop the Kipling story, Fleischman's poem, and the tongue-twister activity, and substitute one or more of the following picture books:

Appelt, Kathi. *Bubbles, Bubbles.* Illustrated by Fumi Kosaka. HarperCollins, 2001.

> This tongue-twisting "fishy, wishy-wash" bath-time experience features a girl and her Ducky and Froggy. The audience members can mime the scrubbing and drying motions. There's a great illustration of the girl with a "scary, hairy do" from her "rubba-dubba pink shampoo."

Baicker, Karen. *Tumble Me Tumbily.* Illustrated by Sam Williams. Handprint Books, 2002.

> A toddler's celebration of waking up and playing all day begins with a bumpity-bump down the stairs with some "bouncity bears." The day ends with a "snuggle me snuggly."

Carlstrom, Nancy White. *Giggle-Wiggle Wake-Up!* Illustrated by Melissa Sweet. Knopf, 2003.

> This is another alliterative celebration for a youngster. Sammy's special day is a "tiny-shiny day," a "tickle-lickle day," "a sniffy-whiffy day," a "silly-willy day," and more.

Fuge, Charles. *Yip! Snap! Yap!* Tricycle, 2001.

> Kids will chime in with the various dog noises culminating in a group "Aroo!" The large two-page spreads feature fun-loving dogs that "Chomp! Munch! Chew!" "Scritch! Scratch! Scruff!" and "Sniffle! Snaffle! Snoo!"

. . . For Fifth and Sixth Graders

Drop the Cronin, Edwards, McCall and Keeler, and Wheeler picture books, and add the following short story:

Vande Velde, Vivian. *The Rumpelstiltskin Problem.* Houghton Mifflin, 2000.

> Saying the name "Rumpelstiltskin" is tricky enough, let alone repeating it several times in the first of several fun retellings by Vivian Vande Velde (even her name is fitting for this theme). Read "A Fairy Tale in Bad Taste." You know it'll be a great selection for this age group from the opening line: "Once upon a time, before pizzerias or Taco Bells, there was a troll named Rumpelstiltskin who began to wonder what a human baby would taste like."

And Yet Even More Clickety-Clackety-Type Titles for You to Consider

Edwards, Pamela Duncan. *Clara Caterpillar.* Illustrated by Henry Cole. HarperCollins, 2001.

————. *Four Famished Foxes and Fosdyke.* Illustrated by Henry Cole. HarperCollins, 1995.

————. *Rosie's Roses.* Illustrated by Henry Cole. HarperCollins, 2003.

Greene, Rhonda Gowler. *Eek! Creak! Snicker, Sneak.* Illustrated by Jos. A. Smith. Atheneum, 2002.

Massie, Diane Redfield. *The Baby BeeBee Bird.* Rev. ed. Illustrated by Steven Kellogg. HarperCollins, 2000.

Mathews, Geda Bradley. *What Was That!* Illustrated by Norman Chartier. Golden, 1977.

Mathews, Judith, and Fay Robinson. *Nathaniel Willy, Scared Silly.* Illustrated by Alexi Natchev. Bradbury, 1994.

Puttock, Simon. *Squeaky Clean.* Illustrated by Mary McQuillan. Little, Brown, 2002.

Van Laan, Nancy. *Teeny Tiny Tingly Tales.* Illustrated by Victoria Chess. Atheneum, 1999.

Wood, Audrey. *Bright and Early Thursday Evening: A Tangled Tale.* Illustrated by Don Wood. Harcourt, 1996.

————. *Silly Sally.* Harcourt, 1992.

THREE

Three

Lesson Plan at a Glance

PICTURE BOOK: *Dusty Locks and the Three Bears* by Susan Lowell

ORAL TALE: "The Bridge" from *Tales from the Brothers Grimm and the Sisters Weird* by Vivian Vande Velde

PICTURE BOOK: *The Three Silly Girls Grubb* by John Hassett and Ann Hassett

CHAPTER BOOK SELECTION: *Three Terrible Trins* by Dick King-Smith

MOVEMENT ACTIVITY: "Three Short-Necked Buzzards" from the recording *Rumble to the Bottom* by Colleen and Uncle Squaty

PICTURE BOOK: *Good Night, Good Knight* by Shelley Moore Thomas

POEM: "Night, Knight"

ACTIVITY: Three-Legged Race and Other "Silly Olympics" Events

Preparation and Presentation

Three is a powerful number in western folklore and many children's stories. This is evident in several popular tales, such as "The Three Little Pigs," "The

Three Billy Goats Gruff," and "The Three Sillies." There are many stories in which three wishes are granted or three sets of brothers or sisters set out to accomplish deeds, many times with the youngest sibling succeeding where the older two failed. Explore the many possibilities of the number three by starting with a fractured version of one of the more familiar stories, "Goldilocks and the Three Bears."

PICTURE BOOK

Lowell, Susan. *Dusty Locks and the Three Bears.* Illustrated by Randy Cecil. Holt, 2001.

This rollicking, western-style version of "Goldilocks and the Three Bears" features a filthy little girl and three grizzly bears. Instead of porridge, the bears have beans. This regional tale has a fun narrative to read aloud: "Someone's been sitting in my chair, and smashed it all to flinders!"

ORAL TALE

Vande Velde, Vivian. "The Bridge." In *Tales from the Brothers Grimm and the Sisters Weird.* Harcourt, 1995.

This is a fun retelling of "The Three Billy Goats Gruff," with a nod to the older crowd. After the biggest goat dispatches the troll, he knocks the other two goats into the water for failing to warn him about the troll.

PICTURE BOOK

Hassett, John, and Ann Hassett. *The Three Silly Girls Grubb.* Houghton Mifflin, 2002.

Three sisters miss the bus and must cross the bridge to get to school in this silly retelling of "The Three Billy Goats Gruff." Instead of a troll, the girls face Ugly-Boy Bobby. In the end, the biggest Grubb girl threatens the boy with "a dozen mushy kisses on your little-boy nose." This sends Ugly-Boy Bobby running to school, where he becomes known as Robert and never misses another day. Instead of the traditional "Snip! Snap! Snout! This tale's told out," the book ends with the chant, "Spink! Spank! Spinach! This story is finished."

CHAPTER BOOK SELECTION

King-Smith, Dick. *Three Terrible Trins.* Crown, 1994.

Read the brief opening chapter, titled "Three Boys," which introduces the mice trins (triplets). Then read the last half of chapter 7, "Exit Wallace."

The trins, their mother, and a mouse named Kevin snap a mousetrap on a cat's tail. Begin with the line, "Mrs. Gray's scheme was indeed a dangerous one," and read until the end of the chapter.

MOVEMENT ACTIVITY

Colleen and Uncle Squaty. "Three Short-Necked Buzzards." In *Rumble to the Bottom* (recording). North Side Music, 1997.

Have everyone stand and stretch to this fun activity.

> Three short-necked buzzards, (*Hold up three fingers and scrunch shoulders.*)
> Three short-necked buzzards, (*Repeat above motions.*)
> Three short-necked buzzards (*Repeat above motions.*)
> Sittin' on a dead tree. (*Make a tree shape with arms.*)
> One flew away. (*Flap arms.*)
> What a shame. (*Shrug and lift hands.*)
> How many left?

Repeat with "Two short-necked buzzards," then "One short-necked buzzard." When you reach "No short-necked buzzards," replace "One flew away / What a shame" with "But one has RE-turned / Let us RE-joice," and work your way back up to "Three short-necked buzzards."

Colleen and Uncle Squaty's recordings may be purchased at www.colleenandunclesquaty.com.

PICTURE BOOK

Thomas, Shelley Moore. *Good Night, Good Knight.* Illustrated by Jennifer Plecas. Dutton, 2000.

"Once there were three little dragons." These three dragons live in a dark cave and ask the Good Knight to bring them a glass of water, read and sing to them, and give them good-night kisses. This book can easily be adapted for a lot of audience participation. Direct them to create and act out the many sounds and motions found throughout the story. When the Good Knight repeatedly hears "a very large, very loud roar," ask the audience to provide this noise. When he climbs up and down the "crumbly, tumbly tower," have them make climbing motions with arms and legs (with lots of panting). When the Good Knight gets on his horse, have the kids raise one arm and shout "Away" and then slap their legs as he "clippety-clops" to the dragons' cave. Once at the cave, the kids can put a finger to their lips and whisper "Good night, good dragon," pantomime drinking a glass of water and making a "glug-glug" sound, hold their palms out as if holding a book, sing to one dragon with some "la-la-la's," blow air kisses, and give a series of final snores.

POEM

"Night, Knight." Anonymous

> "Night, knight,"
> said one knight
> to the other knight
> the other night.
> "Night, night, knight."

ACTIVITY

Three-Legged Race and Other "Silly Olympics" Events

Finish the program with an old-fashioned three-legged race resulting in the awarding of the three Olympic medals—gold, silver, and bronze. Create other "Silly Olympics" events such as "Cotton Ball Shot Put" (see who can throw a cotton ball the farthest), "Plastic Straw Javelin Throw" (contestants either blow the paper wrapper off the straw or toss it into the air like a javelin), and "Balloon Toss" (kids blow up a balloon and release it, waiting to see whose balloon lands the farthest away after it loses its air). These particular contests allow the younger kids to compete against the older kids because strength and size are no advantage. Sometimes the cotton balls, straws, and balloons go two inches (or negative inches) for the big kids and several feet for the smaller kids. Make sure everyone who participates receives an award, such as a paperback book, medal, certificate, sticker, or edible treat.

Mix and Match Picture Books

Fearnley, Jan. *Mr. Wolf and the Three Bears*. Harcourt, 2002.

Mr. Wolf and Grandma throw a celebration for Baby Bear's birthday, but Goldilocks crashes the party and ruins everything. In the end, Grandma bakes a special treat that contains an ingredient that might be too much for the preschool crowd, but the school-age crowd will find it funny and gross.

Gantschev, Ivan. *The Three Little Rabbits*. North-South Books, 2002.

In this Balkan folktale, three rabbits go out into the world. Instead of a burrow, the first rabbit makes a nest, and the second rabbit makes a home out of branches, moss, and leaves. A fox chases them both away. The third rabbit digs a deep, snug burrow in which the fox gets stuck. Ask the audience to compare this story to the popular, traditional "Three Little Pigs" story.

Heine, Helme. *The Most Wonderful Egg in the World*. Atheneum, 1983.

A king tries to settle which of the three hens is the most beautiful. He declares that the hen that lays the most wonderful egg will become a princess. The first hen lays a perfect, white, spotless egg. The second lays the biggest egg the king has ever seen. The third hen lays "an egg that would be talked about for the next hundred years," a square egg with a different color on each surface. (The kids always "ooh" and "ahh" at this point in the story.) As a follow-up craft activity, give the kids a coloring sheet and let them design their own version of the most wonderful egg in the world. As in the book, declare everyone a winner.

Hopkins, Jackie Mims. *The Horned Toad Prince*. Illustrated by Michael Austin. Peachtree, 2000.

This retelling of the traditional story "The Frog Prince" is set in the U.S. Southwest. A horned toad helps young Reba Jo retrieve her sombrero from a well in exchange for "tres pequeños," three small favors. This is both a fun read-aloud for the numerous Spanish phrases and as a companion book to Susan Lowell's *Dusty Locks and the Three Bears* listed in the above lesson plan.

Lester, Helen. *Tackylocks and the Three Bears*. Illustrated by Lynn Munsinger. Houghton Mifflin, 2002.

Tacky the penguin and friends put on their theatrical version of "Goldilocks and the Three Bears." Tacky manages to eat all of the porridge, bust each and every chair, and fall asleep. The penguin chicks in the audience state that it's the best play ever. The illustrations of the penguins in bear headgear are hilarious.

Lester, Helen. *Three Cheers for Tacky*. Illustrated by Lynn Munsinger. Houghton Mifflin, 1994.

Instead of properly performing the cheerleading routine that goes "1, 2, 3, Left! 1, 2, 3, Right! Stand up! Sit down! Say 'Good night,'" Tacky the penguin adds some miscued moves to the delight of the cheerleading-contest judges. Pass out hankies or tissues to simulate pom-poms, and let the audience move along to the various cheerleading routines.

Martin, C. L. G. *Three Brave Women*. Illustrated by Peter Elwell. Atheneum, 1991.

Three generations of females express their fears of spiders. The youngest decides to do something about it, and all three find themselves under the porch, a "perfect spider hangout," in order to catch a spider and overcome their fears. This is a nice, quiet tale of courage.

McAllister, Angela. *Barkus, Sly and the Golden Egg*. Illustrated by Sally Anne Lambert. Bloomsbury, 2002.

Three hens outwit the two foxes that catch them for dinner. The hens convince the foxes that one of the hens is able to lay a golden egg. There are some funny scenes, such as the foxes eating boot stew while waiting for the golden egg and the subsequent "chick that will lay more golden eggs." There are several chances to do fun vocals between the foxes and the defiant hens.

Spinelli, Eileen. *Three Pebbles and a Song*. Illustrated by S. D. Schindler. Dial, 2003.

Moses the mouse gets distracted while his family gathers food for the winter. In the end, Moses helps his family while away the long, cold months with music, dance, and the ability to juggle three pebbles.

Tolhurst, Marilyn. *Somebody and the Three Blairs*. Illustrated by Simone Abel. Orchard, 1991.

Humans Mr. Blair, Mrs. Blair, and Baby Blair take on the role of the three bears, while a bear cub acts as the Goldilocks character. This is my favorite "fractured" adaptation of "Goldilocks and the Three Bears" because of the chance to read Baby Blair's lines, such as "Issa big teddy bear."

Wight, Tamra. *The Three Grumpies*. Illustrated by Ross Collins. Bloomsbury, 2003.

The narrator wakes up on the wrong side of the bed and finds the Grumpies—Grumpy, Grumpier, and Grumpiest—sharing her day with her. Her mother suggests trying to get rid of them, her father tells her to show them how she feels, the bus driver advises that she scare them away, and her teacher says to ignore them. It's not until she laughs at them that they unhappily go away . . . looking for another kid to visit.

Mix and Match Chapter Book Selections

Byars, Betsy. *The Pinballs*. HarperCollins, 1977.

This powerful novel describes three kids trying to cope with their difficult situations and adjusting to a foster home. Read the jaw-dropping opening chapter, where we meet Harvey, whose father ran him over and broke both legs; Thomas J., who was abandoned at a farmhouse; and Carlie, who was hit once too often by her abusive stepfather. Afterward, see how many audience members line up to check out the book.

Manes, Stephen. *Be a Perfect Person in Just Three Days*. Clarion, 1982.

Read the funny first chapter, where the author of the book that Milo discovers in the library warns him not to sneak a look at the last page. When Milo does, he finds the words "Boy, Are You Dumb! Didn't I tell you not to look at the last page of the book?"

McNamee, Graham. *Nothing Wrong with a Three-Legged Dog*. Delacorte, 2000.

Leftovers is a three-legged beagle with an artificial ear. Keith, the only white kid in his class, befriends a biracial girl the kids call Zebra. Read chapter 2, which begins with the sentence, "The first time I saw Lynda she was carrying a shopping bag full of dog turds" (her father is a dog walker and she's on "poop alert"). The entertaining chapter ends with the lines, "That's how I met Lynda and Leftovers and fell in love. With Leftovers, I mean, not Lynda. She's okay, but she's no beagle."

Scieszka, Jon. *Knights of the Kitchen Table*. Viking, 1991.

Introduce the audience to the Time Warp Trio in their very first adventure. Tell the audience that the trio travels back and forth in time, and they have just landed in the time of King Arthur. Read chapter 3, where they confront the Black Knight. The boys find that the Black Knight is easily angered by their taunts. Make a loud "Boingggg" noise when they defeat him with a stick to the helmet.

Mix and Match Oral Tales

Kimmel, Eric. "The Three Riddles." In *Fire and Wings: Dragon Tales from East and West*. Edited by Marianne Carus. Cricket, 2002.

Three soldiers have seven years to answer the three riddles asked of them by a dragon or he will devour them. The answers they seek are to the questions, "What is our meat?" "What is our spoon?" and "What is our wineglass?"

Mix and Match Poetry

Lansky, Bruce. "Three Kind Mice." In *The New Adventures of Mother Goose.* Illustrated by Stephen Carpenter. Meadowbrook, 1993.

Wise, William. "The Awful Three" and "Three Dinosaur Ages." In *Dinosaurs Forever.* Illustrated by Lynn Munsinger. Dial, 2000.

———. "Just Three." In *The Twentieth Century Children's Poetry Treasury.* Edited by Jack Prelutsky. Illustrated by Meilo So. Knopf, 1999; and in *Read-Aloud Rhymes for the Very Young.* Edited by Jack Prelutsky. Illustrated by Marc Brown. Knopf, 1986.

Tweaking the Program Theme . . .

. . . For Preschoolers

Drop the Vande Velde oral tale and the King-Smith chapter book selection, and substitute any "nonfractured" version of "Goldilocks and the Three Bears," "The Three Billy Goats Gruff," or "The Three Little Pigs" or any combination of these stories. It's remarkable how many young children are not exposed to these traditional stories. Teachers and librarians should take any opportunity to share them. Here is a list of well-designed versions of these classics:

GOLDILOCKS AND THE THREE BEARS

Aylesworth, Jim. *Goldilocks and the Three Bears.* Illustrated by Barbara McClintock. Scholastic, 2003.

Brett, Jan. *Goldilocks and the Three Bears.* Dodd, Mead, 1987.

Gorbachev, Valeri. *Goldilocks and the Three Bears.* North-South Books, 2001.

THE THREE BILLY GOATS GRUFF

Carpenter, Stephen. *The Three Billy Goats Gruff.* HarperFestival, 1998.

Finch, Mary. *The Three Billy Goats Gruff.* Barefoot, 2001.

Galdone, Paul. *The Three Billy Goats Gruff.* Clarion, 1973.

Rounds, Glen. *The Three Billy Goats Gruff.* Holiday House, 1993.

THE THREE LITTLE PIGS

Galdone, Paul. *The Three Little Pigs.* Clarion, 1970.

Moser, Barry. *The Three Little Pigs.* Little, Brown, 2001.

Zemach, Margot. *The Three Little Pigs: An Old Story.* Farrar, Straus and Giroux, 1988.

. . . For Fifth and Sixth Graders

Drop the Hassett, Lowell, and Thomas picture books, and substitute the following picture book:

Muth, Jon J. *The Three Questions.* Scholastic, 2002.

> Based on a Leo Tolstoy story, a boy searches for the answers to the following questions: "When is the best time to do things?" "Who is the most important one?" and "What is the right thing to do?" He finds the answers from a heron, a monkey, a dog, a turtle, and a panda.

Add one or more of the following chapter book selections:

Garner, James Finn. *Politically Correct Bedtime Stories.* Macmillan, 1994.

> A lot of this collection will go over your audience's heads, but they will delight in the wordplay. "The Three Codependent Goats Gruff" shows the troll breaking down and blaming himself for the whole incident. "Goldilocks" is now a biologist who specializes in the study of anthropomorphic bears. "The Three Little Pigs" finds the little porkers living "together in mutual respect and in harmony with their environment."

Jacobs, W. W. "The Monkey's Paw." In *The Haunted Looking Glass.* New York Review Books, 2001.

> This much-anthologized short story tells of a little, mummified monkey paw that grants three wishes. Start with the sentence, "What was that you started telling me the other day about a monkey's paw or something, Morris?" If you don't have time to read the entire short story, stop at the end of section two and leave the audience hanging. This is a good story for those in the audience wanting a good shivery story.

And Yet Even More Books Concerning the Number Three for You to Consider

Adams, Georgie. *The Three Little Witches Storybook.* Illustrated by Emily Bolam. Hyperion, 2002.

DeWan, Ted. *Crispin and the Three Little Piglets*. Doubleday, 2002.

Egielski, Richard. *Three Magic Balls*. HarperCollins, 2000.

Johnson, Angela. *One of Three*. Illustrated by David Soman. Orchard, 1991.

Kellogg, Steven. *The Three Sillies*. Candlewick, 1999.

Mahy, Margaret. *The Three-Legged Cat*. Illustrated by Jonathan Allen. Viking, 1993.

Miller, Sara Swan. *Three Stories You Can Read to Your Dog*. Illustrated by True Kelley. Houghton Mifflin, 1995. (First in a series of five books.)

Pfeffer, Beth. *The Trouble with Wishes*. Holt, 1996.

Reiser, Lynn. *Two Mice in Three Fables*. Greenwillow, 1995.

Snyder, Dianne. *The Boy of the Three-Year Nap*. Illustrated by Allen Say. Houghton Mifflin, 1988.

Stamm, Claus. *Three Strong Women*. Illustrated by Jean Tseng and Mou-sien Tseng. Viking, 1990.

Wiesner, David. *The Three Pigs*. Clarion, 2001.

Wood, Audrey. *Three Sisters*. Illustrated by Rosekrans Hoffman. Dial, 1986.

Zemach, Margot. *The Three Wishes*. Farrar, Straus and Giroux, 1986.

FOUR

The Coolest School

Lesson Plan at a Glance

Preparation and Presentation

There are so many stories about school that are definitely more meaningful for the school-age crowd than for preschoolers. The following stories and activities, for the most part (and sometimes in a roundabout way), extol the pleasures of school. Create a Teacher Hall of Fame wall display with poster board cutouts of "cool" storybook teachers, such as Mrs. Frizzle from the Magic School Bus series, Mrs. Jewels of the Wayside School series, and Miss Bindergarten.

PICTURE BOOK

Munsch, Robert. *Show and Tell.* Illustrated by Michael Martchenko. Annick, 1991.

Start off the program with this highly participative picture book. Benjamin takes his baby sister to school for show-and-tell. Baby sister starts to cry, "WAAA, WAAA, WAAA, WAAA, WAAA," over and over again. Teach your audience to "WAAA" like the baby sister. Tell them to cry five "WAAAs" each time—no more, no less. Stress the importance of this, or you will not be able to proceed with the story. Again, I speak from experience. Give them a visual cue to cry, such as wrinkling your face, as a baby does before letting loose with a strong cry. Make a slash or cutoff motion with your hand to stop the "WAAAs."

PICTURE BOOK

Dr. Seuss and Jack Prelutsky. *Hooray for Diffendoofer Day!* Illustrated by Lane Smith. Knopf, 1998.

Diffendoofer School is definitely unique. The teaching staff includes Miss Bobble, Miss Wobble, Miss Fribble, Miss Quibble, and the teacher who is "different-er than the rest," Miss Bonkers. The principal is rumored to take his eyebrows off at night, and the school librarian cries out "louder" to the students when they read to themselves.

CHAPTER BOOK SELECTION

Park, Barbara. *Junie B. Jones and Her Big Fat Mouth.* Random House, 1993.

You could read almost any chapter from any Junie B. Jones book and be a hit with your audience. The last two chapters of this book celebrate a school employee who usually goes unnoticed and unrewarded—the school custodian. The kids in Junie B's class laugh at her when she declares that she wants to be a janitor when she grows up. They change their tune when she brings in the school janitor, Gus Vallony ("Vallony is my favorite kind of sandwich!"), to show-and-tell.

PICTURE BOOK

Creech, Sharon. *A Fine, Fine School.* Illustrated by Harry Bliss. HarperCollins, 2001.

Mr. Keene, the principal, is very proud of the students, the teachers, and the school. He starts scheduling school on Saturdays . . . and then on Sundays . . . and then the holidays . . . and then all summer. The kids finally convince him that as much as they like school, they don't want to go every single day. Share some of the subtle background jokes, such as a dog dressed in baseball catcher's gear and a young boy holding a book titled *This Book Is Way Too Hard for You.*

POEM/READER'S THEATER

Dakos, Kalli. "It's inside My Sister's Lunch." In *If You're Not Here, Please Raise Your Hand: Poems about School.* Illustrated by G. Brian Karas. Simon and Schuster, 1990.

This poem, which tells about a class in which all the children forget their book money, could be viewed as a ready-to-go reader's theater script. There are voices for the teacher and up to thirteen students. In the end, Tim remembers that his money is in his sock. All the other children exclaim together, "The teacher passed out from the shock."

POEM

"I Love to Do My Homework." Anonymous

Share this funny poem to continue the poetry thread started with the reader's theater production and to lead up to the rest of the program.

> I love to do my homework,
> It makes me feel so good.
> I love to do exactly
> As my teacher says I should.
> I love to do my homework,
> I never miss a day.
> I even love the men in white
> Who are taking me away.

CHAPTER BOOK SELECTION

Sachar, Louis. *Wayside School Gets a Little Stranger.* Morrow, 1995.

Read chapter 3, "Poetry." This is one of the funniest stories found in all five

Wayside School books. Mrs. Jewls tells her students to pick a color and write a poem about it. The kids fret and work their way through the assignment. The chapter ends with their finished poems. This selection is a good lead-in to more poetry assignments. Sachar's other four Wayside School books are

More Sideways Arithmetic from Wayside School. Scholastic, 1994.

Sideways Arithmetic from Wayside School. Scholastic, 1989.

Sideways Stories from Wayside School. Morrow, 1978.

Wayside School Is Falling Down. Lothrop, Lee and Shepard, 1989.

POETRY ACTIVITIES

There are a variety of poetry activities that you can use to cap off "The Coolest School" theme. These include two writing exercises or a group reading from the many school poems on the children's book market.

The first writing exercise is to imitate the assignment given to Mrs. Jewls's students. Ask the kids to write their own color poems. This could be done individually or as a group. Introduce the poem "Why the Frog in Our Class Is Purple" from Kalli Dakos's book *Put Your Eyes up Here and Other School Poems* (Simon and Schuster, 2003) as an example.

The second writing exercise is based on Myra Cohen Livingston's book *I Am Writing a Poem About: A Game of Poetry* (Margaret K. McElderry, 1997). Livingston assigns a series of words, and her students must fashion a poem around those words. To fit this theme, you might ask the kids to come up with a poem that contains the words *Teacher, Principal, School,* and *Cool.*

Display many of the school poems available on the market today in your program area, and ask the kids to find some good ones to share with the rest of the audience. Check out the long list of possibilities in the "Mix and Match Poetry" section of this chapter.

Mix and Match Picture Books

Calmenson, Stephanie. *The Teeny Tiny Teacher.* Illustrated by Denis Roche. Scholastic, 1998.

This version of the traditional tale "Teeny Tiny Woman" is set in classroom and school field-trip settings. The teacher finds a "teeny tiny bone for our teeny tiny science lesson." The class soon finds itself haunted by the spectral owner of the bone. Read the many "teeny tinys" in a high-pitched voice, and contrast the final climatic "Take It!" with a powerful, low-pitched roar.

Catalanotto, Peter. *Matthew ABC*. Atheneum, 2002.

Teacher Mrs. Tuttle has a unique method of telling her twenty-five Matthews apart. Many are hilarious, such as "Matthew G. has trouble with glue," and the audience sees an illustration of paper, crayons, scissors, a cup, and a chair all stuck to the little boy.

Falconer, Ian. *Olivia Saves the Circus*. Atheneum, 2001.

Olivia tells her class about her vacation. "Olivia always blossoms in front of an audience." Her teacher is not totally pleased with the tall tales that come out of Olivia's mouth.

London, Jonathan. *Froggy Goes to School*. Illustrated by Frank Remkiewicz. Viking, 1996.

Froggy goes to the first day of school in his underwear. It's only a dream. His real first day of school turns out to be a success.

Plourde, Lynn. *Teacher Appreciation Day*. Illustrated by Thor Wickstrom. Dutton, 2003.

Maybella Jean Wishywashy can't make up her mind how to show her appreciation for her teacher, Mrs. Shepard. She tries a bit too hard, but in the end, she showers her teacher with plenty of appreciation.

Polacco, Patricia. *Mr. Lincoln's Way*. Philomel, 2001.

His students think Mr. Lincoln is "the coolest principal in the whole world." He sets out to help Mean Gene, the school bully.

Pulver, Robin. *Axle Annie*. Illustrated by Tedd Arnold. Dial, 1999.

Axle Annie is the coolest and most dedicated school bus driver. Nothing will stop her from getting the kids to school. This upsets Shifty Rhodes, a school bus driver who complains to the Grouch and Grump Club that he wants to stay home for a snow day.

Roche, Denis. *The Best Class Picture Ever!* Scholastic, 2003.

Elvis the hamster, the class pet, is missing for the class picture, and everyone is upset. The photographer, Mr. Click, is patient and keeps the class occupied while the teacher searches for Elvis (who is visible to the astute reader). Mr. Click asks the kids for a new word to use in place of the traditional *cheese* to induce smiles. Suggestions include *hiccups, feet, moustache, underwear,* and the eventual winner—*trombone*.

Slate, Joseph. *Miss Bindergarten Stays Home from Kindergarten.* Illustrated by Ashley Wolff. Dutton, 2000.

Even fourth graders will enjoy hearing about Miss Bindergarten, the famous kindergarten teacher. The class enjoys substitute teacher Mr. Tusky (he's an elephant), but the students still miss their regular teacher, who is home with the flu. One by one, the students get sick. The story ends with the line, "On Saturday and Sunday, everybody stays home from kindergarten . . . especially Mr. Tusky" (who is shown sick in bed).

Other books in Slate's Miss Bindergarten series include

> *Miss Bindergarten Celebrates the 100th Day of Kindergarten.* Dutton, 1998.
>
> *Miss Bindergarten Gets Ready for Kindergarten.* Dutton, 1996.
>
> *Miss Bindergarten Plans a Circus with Kindergarten.* Dutton, 2002.
>
> *Miss Bindergarten Takes a Field Trip with Kindergarten.* Dutton, 2001.

Mix and Match Reader's Theater

Aaron Shepard has developed a funny adaptation from Louis Sachar's *Sideways Stories from Wayside School* on his web site: www.aaronshep.com. The script is titled "Three Sideways Stories from Wayside School" and may be copied and performed for noncommercial purposes. The script calls for nine readers (Mrs. Jewls, Joe, Bebe, Calvin, Louis, and four narrators). The three stories are based on the following chapters: "Joe," in which Mrs. Jewls tries to teach Joe how to count the "correct" way; "Bebe," who thinks that quantity is more important than quality when it comes to art; and "Calvin," who is told to deliver a note to an imaginary teacher.

Mix and Match Poetry

The following volumes contain either all school-themed poems or include an entire section on school poems.

Dakos, Kalli. *The Bug in Teacher's Coffee and Other School Poems.* Illustrated by Mike Reed. HarperCollins, 1999.

―――. *Don't Read This Book Whatever You Do: More Poems about School.* Illustrated by G. Brian Karas. Simon and Schuster, 1993.

———. *The Goof Who Invented Homework: And Other School Poems.* Illustrated by Denise Brunkus. Dial, 1996.

———. *If You're Not Here, Please Raise Your Hand: Poems about School.* Illustrated by G. Brian Karas. Simon and Schuster, 1990.

———. *Mrs. Cole on an Onion Roll: And Other School Poems.* Illustrated by JoAnne Adinolfi. Simon and Schuster, 1995.

———. *Put Your Eyes up Here and Other School Poems.* Illustrated by G. Brian Karas. Simon and Schuster, 2003.

Lansky, Bruce. *A Bad Case of the Giggles: Kids' Favorite Funny Poems, Book #2.* Illustrated by Stephen Carpenter. Meadowbrook, 1994.

———. *If Pigs Could Fly and Other Deep Thoughts.* Illustrated by Stephen Carpenter. Meadowbrook, 2000.

———. *Kids Pick the Funniest Poems.* Illustrated by Stephen Carpenter. Meadowbrook, 1991.

———. *No More Homework! No More Tests! Kids' Favorite Funny School Poems.* Illustrated by Stephen Carpenter. Meadowbrook, 1997.

———. *Poetry Party.* Illustrated by Stephen Carpenter. Meadowbrook, 1996.

Lillegard, Dee. *Hello School! A Classroom Full of Poems.* Illustrated by Don Carter. Knopf, 2001.

Shields, Carol Diggery. *Almost Late to School: And More School Poems.* Illustrated by Paul Meisel. Dutton, 2003.

———. *Lunch Money and Other Poems about School.* Illustrated by Paul Meisel. Dutton, 1995.

Sierra, Judy. *There's a Zoo in Room 22.* Illustrated by Barney Saltzberg. Harcourt, 2000.

Taberski, Sharon. *Morning, Noon and Night: Poems to Fill Your Day.* Illustrated by Nancy Doniger. Mondo, 1996.

The following individual school-related poems have also been big hits with kids:

Crossen, Stacy Jo, and Natalie Ann Covell. "Wiggly Giggles." In *The Random House Book of Poetry for Children.* Edited by Jack Prelutsky. Illustrated by Arnold Lobel. Random House, 1983.

Kennedy, X. J. "Mixed-Up School." In *Exploding Gravy: Poems to Make You Laugh.* Illustrated by Joy Allen. Little, Brown, 2002.

McNaughton, Colin. "I Thought I'd Take My Rat to School. In *For Laughing Out Loud: Poems to Tickle Your Funnybone*. Edited by Jack Prelutsky. Illustrated by Marjorie Priceman. Knopf, 1991.

Proimos, James. "Don't Hate Me Because I'm the Teacher's Pet" and "Happy Song." In *If I Were in Charge the Rules Would Be Different*. Scholastic, 2002.

Silverstein, Shel. "Crazy Dream." In *Falling Up*. HarperCollins,1996.

———. "Homework Machine." In *A Light in the Attic*. HarperCollins, 1981.

———."Kidnapped." In *A Light in the Attic*. HarperCollins, 1981.

Soto, Gary. "Eraser and School Clock" and "My Teacher in the Market." In *Canto Familiar*. Illustrated by Annika Nelson. Harcourt, 1995.

Stevenson, James. "Classroom." In *Just around the Corner*. Greenwillow, 2001.

Viorst, Judith. "First Day of School." In *Sad Underwear and Other Complications*. Illustrated by Richard Hull. Atheneum, 1995.

Whitehead, Jenny. "The 1st Day of School," "The 179th Day of School," and "It's Off to Kindergarten." In *Lunch Box Mail and Other Poems*. Holt, 2001.

Tweaking the Program Theme . . .

. . . For Preschoolers

Drop the Creech and Seuss and Prelutsky picture books, the Sachar chapter book selection, and the poetry activities, and substitute the following picture books:

Bloom, Suzanne. *The Bus for Us*. Boyds Mill, 2001.

> While waiting for the school bus, a girl and her brother see a variety of vehicles, such as an ice cream truck, a tow truck, and a taxi.

Numeroff, Laura Joffe. *If You Take a Mouse to School*. Illustrated by Felicia Bond. HarperCollins, 2002.

> Numeroff's famous mouse joins the fun at school in the trademark cumulative format.

Shannon, David. *David Goes to School*. Scholastic, 1999.

> The star of Shannon's David series finds his favorite word "NO!" is used a lot in school.

. . . For Fifth and Sixth Graders

Drop the Park chapter book selection, and substitute the following:

Clements, Andrew. *The Janitor's Boy.* Simon and Schuster, 2000.

> Read the opening chapter, where Jack becomes a school vandal by smearing a blob of thirteen pieces of gum on the underside of a school desk. The chapter ends with the audience learning that the school janitor, the person who will have to clean up the mess, is Jack's father. Encourage the kids to read the rest of the book to find out why Jack does such a despicable thing to his father.

And Yet Even More Titles Featuring Cool Schools, Cool Teachers, Cool Principals, and, of Course, Cool Students for You to Consider

Carter, Alden. *Dustin's Big School Day.* Whitman, 1999.

Helakoski, Leslie. *The Smushy Bus.* Illustrated by Salvatore Murdocca. Millbrook, 2002.

London, Jonathan. *Froggy's First Kiss.* Illustrated by Frank Remkiewicz. Viking, 1998.

Munsch, Robert. *Get Out of Bed.* Illustrated by Alan Daniel and Lea Daniel. Scholastic, 1998.

Noble, Trinka Hakes. *Jimmy's Boa and the Bungee Jump Slam Dunk.* Illustrated by Steven Kellogg. Dial, 2003.

Ormerod, Jan. *Ms. MacDonald Has a Class.* Clarion, 1996.

Pulver, Robin. *Mrs. Toggle's Zipper.* Illustrated by R. W. Alley. Four Winds, 1990.

Reynolds, Peter H. *The Dot.* Candlewick, 2003.

Wells, Rosemary. *When I Grow Up.* Illustrated by Rosemary Wells and Jody Wheeler. Hyperion, 2002.

Wolff, Patricia Rae. *The Toll-Bridge Troll.* Illustrated by Kimberly Bulcken Root. Harcourt, 1995.

Wood, Douglas. *What Teachers Can't Do.* Illustrated by Doug Cushman. Simon and Schuster, 2002.

Wright, Betty Ren. *The Blizzard.* Illustrated by Ron Himler. Holiday House, 2003.

FIVE

I Don't Wanna
Go to School!

Lesson Plan at a Glance

POEM:	"Morning Announcements" from *No More Homework! No More Tests! Kids' Favorite Funny School Poems* by Bruce Lansky
PICTURE BOOK:	*First Day Jitters* by Julie Danneberg
SONG:	"I Don't Wanna Go to School" from the recording *Teacher's Favorites* by Barry Louis Polisar
POEM:	"I Do Not Wish to Go to School" from *A Pizza the Size of the Sun* by Jack Prelutsky
CHAPTER BOOK SELECTION:	*Jake Drake, Class Clown* by Andrew Clements
POEM:	"Ms. Stein" by Bill Dodds from *Kids Pick the Funniest Poems*, edited by Bruce Lansky
PICTURE BOOK:	*Crazy Hair Day* by Barney Saltzberg
PICTURE BOOK/READER'S THEATER:	*Fox at School* by Edward Marshall
CHAPTER BOOK SELECTION:	*Three Rotten Eggs* by Gregory Maguire
ACTIVITY:	The Name Change-O-Chart from *Captain Underpants and the Perilous Plot of Professor Poopypants* by Dav Pilkey
POEM:	"Class Dismissed" from *No More Homework! No More Tests! Kids' Favorite Funny School Poems* by Bruce Lansky

Preparation and Presentation

Before the program begins, add the Teacher Hall of Shame to your Teacher Hall of Fame from "The Coolest School" program (chapter 4). Place pictures or cutouts of infamous teachers and principals from children's literature, including Ms. Stein from Dodds's poem, Miss Trunchbull from Dahl's book *Matilda*, Passen's Miss Irma Birmbaum (see these last two in the "Mix and Match" sections), and even Brown's Mr. Ratburn (even though he's not a really bad guy).

POEM

Lansky, Bruce. "Morning Announcements." In *No More Homework! No More Tests! Kids' Favorite Funny School Poems*. Illustrated by Stephen Carpenter. Meadowbrook, 1997.

The voice over the PA system states that "some teachers were suspended for giving too much work," that students will be paid to attend school, cockroach sandwiches will be featured in the cafeteria, and, by the way, April Fool! Roll up a piece of paper and speak into it to imitate the sound of the PA system. Add sound-effect crackles and static noises for fun.

PICTURE BOOK

Danneberg, Julie. *First Day Jitters*. Illustrated by Judy Love. Charlesbridge, 2000.

Sarah pulls the covers over her head and insists that she is not going to school. She is very nervous about the whole idea. We never see her face during the course of the book until we finally learn that Sarah is actually the new teacher.

SONG

Polisar, Barry Louis. "I Don't Wanna Go to School." In *Teacher's Favorites* (recording). Rainbow Morning Music, 1993.

This song is a nice match with the Danneberg picture book. Tommy insists that he is not going to school because everyone is mean and nobody likes him. His mother tells him that he has to go. We learn that Tommy is the school principal. The chorus is catchy, and the kids will be singing along: "I don't wanna go to school." The recording is available from Polisar's web site: www.barrylou.com.

POEM

Prelutsky, Jack. "I Do Not Wish to Go to School." In *A Pizza the Size of the Sun*. Illustrated by James Stevenson. Greenwillow, 1996.

A girl threatens to "eat a worm or two" if her mother makes her go to school. The wise mother obliges by dangling some worms in front of her daughter. The girl replies, "I have changed my mind." Dangle a gummy worm or two as a prop.

CHAPTER BOOK SELECTION

Clements, Andrew. *Jake Drake, Class Clown*. Simon and Schuster, 2002.

Jake's personal mission is to make his overly serious student teacher, Miss Bruce, lighten up and smile. Read chapter 3. Jake intentionally disrupts the excessively strict class spelling bee by spelling "mouse" as "m-i-c-k-e-y."

POEM

Dodds, Bill. "Ms. Stein." In *Kids Pick the Funniest Poems*. Edited by Bruce Lansky. Illustrated by Stephen Carpenter. Meadowbrook, 1991.

Read this poem about a Frankenstein-like substitute teacher who terrifies the students so much that the school bully wets his pants. After hearing about Ms. Stein, kids won't think that their real-life substitute teachers are so bad after all.

PICTURE BOOK

Saltzberg, Barney. *Crazy Hair Day*. Candlewick, 2003.

Stanley gets his hair gelled, sprayed bright orange and blue, and wrapped in spikes for his school's Crazy Hair Day celebration. Unfortunately, Crazy Hair Day is "next Friday." Today is actually School Picture Day!

PICTURE BOOK/READER'S THEATER

Marshall, Edward. *Fox at School*. Illustrated by James Marshall. Dial, 1983.

Adapt a script from the third short story in this collection, "Fox in Charge." Fox declares that he will be a teacher when he grows up. "It's an easy job," he says. When he's placed in charge of the class while his teacher is out, the other students act up. Fox quickly learns that teaching is harder than it looks. There are parts for one narrator, Fox, Miss Moon (the teacher), Mr. Sweet (the principal), and students Carmen, Dexter, Junior, and Betty (the latter two can read the joint statements made by the entire class).

CHAPTER BOOK SELECTION

Maguire, Gregory. *Three Rotten Eggs.* Clarion, 2002.

> Read chapter 3, "Thud Tweed." It contains a very cheeky scene featuring the appearance of the tough new student Thaddeus Nero Tweed, aka Thud (his initials are T.N.T.). Thud manages to humorously insult the rest of the students as they introduce themselves one by one. Begin with the sentence, "I'm looking for Earth's class."

ACTIVITY

The Name Change-O-Chart

Pilkey, Dav. *Captain Underpants and the Perilous Plot of Professor Poopypants.* Scholastic, 2000.

> Professor Poopypants thought that being a teacher was a noble ambition, but when his students laughed at his name (his middle initial stands for Peepee), he goes crazy and develops the name-changer device. Give members of the audience their new names. The book has a chart that assigns new names, or you can use the Scholastic web site chart (www.scholastic.com/captainunderpants/namechanger.htm), which automatically alters each person's name. The chart substitutes new first, middle, and last names. My name, Rob Reid, becomes Loopy Gizzard Nose (which is not as bad as some of the names created). I have shared this activity with my university children's literature classes, and many students have returned their quizzes and tests with their new Name Change-O-Chart names.

POEM

Lansky, Bruce. "Class Dismissed." *No More Homework! No More Tests! Kids' Favorite Funny School Poems.* Illustrated by Stephen Carpenter. Meadowbrook, 1997.

> Ask everyone to stand and sing this poem to the tune of "The Battle Hymn of the Republic." "Glory, glory hallelujah! / School is closed, what's it to ya?"

Mix and Match Picture Books

Calmenson, Stephanie. *The Frog Principal.* Illustrated by Denise Brunkus. Scholastic, 2001.

> In this retelling of the traditional story "The Frog Prince," Mr. Bundy, the school principal, is turned into a frog by an incompetent magician. Mr.

Bundy remains the principal, even in his frog transformation. The kids are generally cool with the idea, except when Mr. Bundy swallows Nancy's bug collection. "The principal ate my homework!"

Cuyler, Margery. *100th Day Worries.* Illustrated by Arthur Howard. Simon and Schuster, 2000.

Jessica frets about the class assignment to bring 100 items of anything to celebrate the 100th day of the school year. Her family finally pitches in and helps her collect "100 bits of love."

DePaola, Tomie. *Trouble in the Barkers' Class.* Putnam, 2003.

New student Carol Anne causes trouble right away despite her new classmates' efforts to make her feel welcome. She cuts to the head of the line, ruins another student's artwork and steals his book, and manages to insult everyone else.

Henkes, Kevin. *Lilly's Purple Plastic Purse.* Greenwillow, 1996.

Lilly loves school and her teacher, Mr. Slinger. One day Lilly disrupts the class, and Mr. Slinger takes away her purse, glasses, and shiny quarters. She is very angry with him until she discovers that he slipped her a note: "Today was a difficult day. Tomorrow will be better." She feels so guilty that she "decided to sit in the uncooperative chair."

Lindbergh, Reeve. *The Awful Aardvarks Go to School.* Illustrated by Tracey Campbell Pearson. Viking, 1997.

A group of young aardvarks attend school and wreak havoc: "They broke every rule." They are truly awful. This rhyming alphabet story is fun to read aloud: "Bullied the Bunny (they pulled down his pants)."

Munsch, Robert. *Stephanie's Ponytail.* Illustrated by Michael Martchenko. Annick, 1996.

This is one of Munsch's funniest books (and that's saying a lot). Stephanie gets very upset when her classmates first insult her various hairstyles, then show up in school wearing the exact same hairstyles.

Passen, Lisa. *Attack of the Fifty-Foot Teacher.* Holt, 2000.

Miss Irma Birmbaum proves that she is the toughest teacher in town by giving homework on Halloween. An encounter with an alien spaceship turns her into an even bigger menace to her students.

Mix and Match Chapter Book Selections

Dahl, Roald. *Matilda.* Illustrated by Quentin Blake. Viking, 1988.

> Is there a meaner principal than Miss Trunchbull? Read the chapter titled "Throwing the Hammer." Matilda and her classmates witness Trunchbull twirling a little girl by the pigtails right over the playground fence. It's a fairly lengthy reading, but Dahl's playful dialogue will keep the audience captivated.

MacDonald, Amy. *No More Nasty.* Farrar, Straus and Giroux, 2001.

> Simon's class has a very unusual substitute teacher. Unfortunately, it's Simon's wacky Aunt Mattie. Simon is embarrassed that his classmates will learn that he's related to this "fruitcake." Read two chapters, "The Secret Weapon" and "To Bee or Not to Be." The students learn "Uncle Philbert's Patented Homework-Reducing Time-Saving Three-Step Multiple-Digit Multiplication Method." This helps Simon's class win a school contest. The actual math formula is clearly explained in the book. Let the audience members try it out.

Naylor, Phyllis Reynolds. *Alice in Blunderland.* Atheneum, 2003.

> Fourth grader Alice feels like a "blunderbuss—a person who goofs up." Read chapter 1, "Being Perfect." In short order, Alice is locked in a bathroom stall, the neighbor boy see her underpants, she sneezes with a mouthful of beans, and her friend embarrasses her by pointing to a chocolate stain on her homework and saying, "What's this? Poop?"

Park, Barbara. *Junie B. Jones Has a Monster under Her Bed.* Random House, 1997.

> Read the hilarious first chapter. The irrepressible Junie has a tough time getting her picture taken by the Cheese Man. He makes the kids say *cheese* when he takes their pictures, and Junie begins to argue with him.

Sachar, Louis. *Marvin Redpost: Alone in His Teacher's House.* Random House, 1994.

> Marvin is dogsitting for his teacher when, to his horror, the dog dies. Read chapter 4, "The Substitute." Marvin finds himself in his substitute teacher's "doghouse."

Mix and Match Poetry

Consider the same sources found in the "Mix and Match Poetry" section of chapter 4, "The Coolest School," and the following individual poems:

Bolsta, Phil. "Michael O'Toole." In *Kids Pick the Funniest Poems*. Edited by Bruce Lansky. Illustrated by Stephen Carpenter. Meadowbrook, 1991.

Dotlich, Rebecca Kai. "Today Is Not a Good Day." In *A Bad Case of the Giggles*. Edited by Bruce Lansky. Illustrated by Stephen Carpenter. Meadowbrook, 1994.

Fatchen, Max. "Look Out." In *Kids Pick the Funniest Poems*. Edited by Bruce Lansky. Illustrated by Stephen Carpenter. Meadowbrook, 1991; in *Knock at a Star*. Rev. ed. Edited by X. J Kennedy and Dorothy M. Kennedy. Illustrated by Karen Lee Baker. Little, Brown, 1999; and in *For Laughing Out Loud*. Edited by Jack Prelutsky. Illustrated by Marjorie Priceman. Knopf, 1991.

Florian, Douglas. "Gum Drop" and "Substitute." In *Laugh-eteria*. Harcourt, 1999.

———. "Three Words." In *Summersaults*. Greenwillow, 2002. (Those three words are "Back to school.")

Harrison, Gregory. "Distracted, the Mother Said to the Boy." In *A Bad Case of the Giggles*. Edited by Bruce Lansky. Illustrated by Stephen Carpenter. Meadowbrook, 1994.

Lansky, Bruce. "My Dog Chewed Up My Homework." In *Poetry Party*. Illustrated by Stephen Carpenter. Meadowbrook, 1996.

Prelutsky, Jack. "Homework! Oh, Homework!" In *The New Kid on the Block*. Illustrated by James Stevenson. Greenwillow, 1984.

———. "A Remarkable Adventure." In *Something Big Has Been Here*. Illustrated by James Stevenson. Greenwillow, 1990.

Silverstein, Shel. "Obedient." In *Falling Up*. HarperCollins, 1996.

———."Sick." In *Where the Sidewalk Ends*. HarperCollins, 1974.

Viorst, Judith. "First Day of School." In *Sad Underwear and Other Complications*. Illustrated by Richard Hull. Atheneum, 1995.

Tweaking the Program Theme . . .

. . . For Preschoolers

Drop the Clements and Maguire chapter book selections, and substitute the following picture books:

Harris, Robie. *I Am Not Going to School Today!* Illustrated by Jan Ormerod. Margaret K. McElderry, 2003.

A little boy doesn't want to go to the first day of school because he's afraid that he doesn't know anything (but he'll go the second day, when "you know everything").

Wells, Rosemary. *Edward Unready for School*. Dial, 1995.

Edward is not quite ready to attend school, despite efforts by his parents, teacher, and classmates. His parents agree to take him back home "until he is ready." This is a reassuring book not only for those kids who need a little extra time to go on to a "next stage" in their life, but also for other kids to see what it's like for their friends who are "unready."

. . . Fifth and Sixth Graders

Drop the Danneberg picture book, and substitute the following chapter book selection:

Koss, Amy. *The Cheat*. Dial, 2003.

Several eighth graders are caught cheating on their midterm exam. Each chapter is told in a different student's voice. Read the first three chapters, "Sarah," "Katie," and "Rob." Sarah sets up the fact that some guy gave her the answers. Katie uses a mnemonic device of singing the answers to the tune of "Row, Row, Row Your Boat." Rob is horrified that their cheating code might be wrong. Skip ahead to the third "Rob" chapter. The students are told to report to the office. End with the third "Sarah" chapter, which ends with her heading into the principal's office.

And Yet Even More Titles about the Horrors of School for You to Consider

Allard, Harry. *Miss Nelson Is Missing*. Illustrated by James Marshall. Houghton Mifflin, 1977.

Brown, Marc. *Arthur's Teacher Moves In*. Little, Brown, 2000.

———. *Arthur's Teacher Troubles*. Little, Brown, 1986.

DeClements, Barthe. *Nothing's Fair in Fifth Grade*. Viking, 1981.

Henkes, Kevin. *Chrysanthemum*. Greenwillow, 1991.

Herman, Gail. *I've Got the Back-to-School Blues*. Illustrated by Stacy Peterson. Grosset and Dunlap, 2002.

Levine, Ellen. *I Hate English!* Illustrated by Steve Bjorkman. Scholastic, 1989.

McKenna, Colleen O'Shaughnessy. *Third Grade Stinks*. Holiday House, 2001.

Munsch, Robert. *Get out of Bed.* Illustrated by Alan Daniel and Lea Daniel. Scholastic, 1998.

O'Neill, Alexis. *The Recess Queen.* Illustrated by Laura Huliska. Scholastic, 2002.

Robinson, Barbara. *The Best School Year Ever.* HarperCollins, 1994.

Russo, Marisabina. *I Don't Want to Go to School.* Greenwillow, 1994.

SIX

Alien Space School

Lesson Plan at a Glance

PICTURE BOOK/WRITING ACTIVITY: *Baloney (Henry P.)* by Jon Scieszka

CHAPTER BOOK SELECTION: *Captain Underpants and the Invasion of the Incredibly Naughty Cafeteria Ladies from Outer Space* by Dav Pilkey

POEM: "School Lunch" from *Laugh-eteria* by Douglas Florian

PICTURE BOOK: *First Graders from Mars, Episode 1: Horus's Horrible Day* by Shana Corey

CHAPTER BOOK SELECTION: *Aliens Don't Carve Jack-O'-Lanterns* by Debbie Dadey and Marcia Thornton Jones

POEM: "Alien Lullaby" from *Laugh-eteria* by Douglas Florian

PICTURE BOOK/ CRAFT AND GAME ACTIVITIES: *George Hogglesberry: Grade School Alien* by Sarah Wilson

CRAFT/DRAWING ACTIVITY: Creating Spaceships and Aliens

Preparation and Presentation

This program theme is the third of this book's school-related story programs (along with chapter 4, "The Coolest School," and chapter 5, "I Don't Wanna Go to School!"). These stories feature the many extraterrestrials that keep showing up in the school system and other friendly, and not-so-friendly, characters from space. Add to the Teacher and Principal Hall of Fame and Hall of Shame with characters from the books used in this program, such as Henry P.'s teacher and Principal Krupp, aka Captain Underpants. Begin the program by welcoming the audience in a robotic-alien voice. Drop hints to indicate that an alien has replaced the regular storyteller. Keep up this routine between stories, but it will grow tiresome and distracting if you use this voice during the stories. (Can I mention one more time that I speak from experience?)

PICTURE BOOK/WRITING ACTIVITY

Scieszka, Jon. *Baloney (Henry P.)*. Illustrated by Lane Smith. Viking, 2001.

An alien student spins a tall tale to avoid "Permanent Lifelong Detention" for being late. This fun picture book to read aloud uses what first appears to be made-up lingo, but actually Scieszka uses "a combination of many Earth languages." Take the time to go back and reexamine these terms with the audience. Make time for the kids to peruse some dictionaries and find other words that are new to them. Lead a short brainstorming session to use these words within the concept of the Scieszka book.

CHAPTER BOOK SELECTION

Pilkey, Dav. *Captain Underpants and the Invasion of the Incredibly Naughty Cafeteria Ladies from Outer Space*. Scholastic, 1999.

Even though the kids don't need to be introduced to the Captain Underpants stories, they still love to hear a grown-up read them. When the school lunch ladies quit in protest of Harold and George's pranks, evil aliens become the new cafeteria workers. Read chapters 9 to 12. The aliens are busy turning the schoolchildren into broken-eyeglasses-held-together-with-masking-tape, pocket-protector-type nerds.

POEM

Florian, Douglas. "School Lunch." In *Laugh-eteria*. Harcourt, 1999.

The narrator feels that the "school lunch is from outer space." For example, the spinach causes gangrene. As bad as the food appears to be, the narrator still feels that lunch is the best part of school.

PICTURE BOOK

Corey, Shana. *First Graders from Mars, Episode 1: Horus's Horrible Day.*
Illustrated by Mark Teague. Scholastic, 2001.

Horus has trouble adjusting to first grade after "martiangarten." He learns
to help Pelly, a new student from the moon Phobos, adjust to the new
school. The book includes a funny scene where Horus's mother gives him a
good-bye kiss and leaves behind a red suction mark.

CHAPTER BOOK SELECTION

Dadey, Debbie, and Marcia Thornton Jones. *Aliens Don't Carve Jack-O'-
Lanterns.* Scholastic, 2002.

The popular Bailey School kids believe that Mr. Spark, a professional party
planner, is an alien from the planet Liron who plans to steal all of Earth's
candy supply. Read chapters 4 to 6. Mr. Spark instructs the students to decorate the school gym for a Halloween party. His new rule is that the students
must bring candy instead of expecting to receive some. When the kids hit
town, they discover that all of the stores are out of sweets. This book comes
with several puzzles and recipes, such as apple dip and no-bake cookies.
Consider using them as optional activities to incorporate into the program.
Other titles in the series that deal with aliens include

Aliens Don't Wear Braces. Scholastic, 1993.

Martians Don't Take Temperatures. Scholastic, 1996.

Mrs. Jeepers in Outer Space. Scholastic, 1999.

POEM

Florian, Douglas. "Alien Lullaby." In *Laugh-eteria.* Harcourt, 1999.

This short, funny ditty encourages the little alien to lay down its three
heads.

PICTURE BOOK/CRAFT AND GAME ACTIVITIES

Wilson, Sarah. *George Hogglesberry: Grade School Alien.* Illustrated by Chad
Cameron. Tricycle, 2001.

A new student from the planet Frollop II tries very hard to fit into his new
class on Earth. Although the book is strange, it's still oddly appealing to kids.
The front jacket flap includes a pattern for George's fake nose. Reproduce

these, and let students cut, color, and wear their own fake noses. The flap copy also suggests taping the book jacket on a wall and playing Pin the Nose on George's Face. This takes "interactive books" to a new extreme.

CRAFT/DRAWING ACTIVITY

Creating Spaceships and Aliens

Let the audience members "gravitate" toward a drawing station filled with paper and drawing materials or a craft station. The following resource books will inspire the young artists:

> Ames, Lee. *Draw Fifty Airplanes, Aircraft, and Spacecraft*. Doubleday, 1977.
>
> Ames, Lee. *Draw Fifty Aliens, UFOs, Galaxy Ghouls, Milky Way Marauders, and Other Extraterrestrial Creatures*. Doubleday, 1998.
>
> Barr, Steve. *1-2-3 Draw Cartoon Aliens and Space Stuff*. Peel Productions, 2003.

Set out building supplies, such as paper, tape, glue, and scissors, and the following resources for those young crafters:

> Blocksma, Mary, and Dewey Blocksma. *Easy-to-Make Spaceships That Really Fly*. Illustrated by Marisabina Russo. Simon and Schuster, 1983.
>
> Ross, Kathy. *Crafts for Kids Who Are Wild about Outer Space*. Illustrated by Sharon Lane Holm. Millbrook, 1997.

Consider soliciting funds from Friends groups, the PTA, and other supporting organizations to purchase copies of the following resource book designed for the kids to cut up and assemble:

> Grater, Michael. *Cut and Fold Paper Spaceships That Fly*. Dover, 1981.

You can't beat the price tag of $3.95.

Mix and Match Picture Books

Cazet, Denys. *Minnie and Moo and the Potato from Planet X*. HarperCollins, 2002.

A potato-shaped alien named Spud crash-lands in Minnie and Moo's pasture. The two cows try to help Spud return to space and stop Earth from bumping into other planets. Spud's spaceship requires a special type of fuel—milk—which Minnie sheepishly provides.

Johnston, Tony. *Alien and Possum: Friends No Matter What*. Simon and
Schuster, 2001.

In the spirit of Arnold Lobel's Frog and Toad books, these stories concern
the unlikeliest of friends. Alien crash-lands in Possum's woods, and the two
develop a very unusual relationship. The first story in the trilogy sets up
their situation. The second story finds Alien upset with a trash can that
doesn't respond with a "hello." The third story is the funniest. Possum
wants Alien to help him stay awake. Alien pinches and puts ice down
Possum's pajamas. Their stories continue in Johnston's sequel:

Alien and Possum: Hanging Out. Simon and Schuster, 2002.

Layton, Neal. *Smile If You're Human*. Dial, 1999.

An alien child and its parents land on Earth hoping to take a picture of a
human. They land inside a zoo. The young alien wonders if the various animals are the humans it seeks. He finally snaps a photo of what he believes
is a human and what the reader knows is an ape.

Pinkwater, Daniel. *Guys from Space*. Macmillan, 1989.

After getting permission from his mother, the young narrator goes up into
space with a bunch of greenish yellow space guys. They land on another
planet and discover root-beer floats. The space guys are so excited about the
possibility of adding ice cream to root beer that they rush our narrator home
before heading back to their home planet. This silly story is told in simple
sentences as if a child wrote it.

Reiser, Lynn. *Earthdance*. Greenwillow, 1999.

Terra's mother is an astronaut. Mom blasts off into space to get a space picture for Terra's school show. The illustrations combine watercolor paints
with actual NASA photographs.

Mix and Match Chapter Book Selections

Coville, Bruce. *Aliens Ate My Homework*. Minstrel, 1993.

Rod Allbright is enlisted to help miniature aliens capture an interstellar
criminal. Read chapter 8, "Temporal Disruption." The school bully takes a
swing at Rod to start off the chapter: "Arnie's fist was heading straight for
my nose." The chapter continues with Rod explaining to his teacher that an

alien ate his math homework. The chapter ends when Rod's mother enters his bedroom and picks up one of the aliens.

Coville, Bruce. *My Teacher Is an Alien*. Minstrel, 1989.

Coville's book is the first in one of the most popular science fiction series for children of all time. Susan dislikes Mr. Smith, her new teacher. When he mistakenly picks up a nasty note that Susan wrote about him, she decides to sneak into his house and retrieve it. Read chapter 4, "Broxholm." Susan hears awful noises coming from Smith's house. She watches in horror as Smith, aka Broxholm, removes his face. The chapter ends with the line, "he had come to earth to kidnap kids and take them into space!" The other books in Coville's series are

> *My Teacher Flunked the Planet*. Minstrel, 1992.
>
> *My Teacher Fried My Brains*. Minstrel, 1991.
>
> *My Teacher Glows in the Dark*. Minstrel, 1991.

Korman, Gordon. *Nose Pickers from Outer Space*. Hyperion, 1999.

Devin Hunter is mortified to learn that the new exchange student living with his family is a total nerd. Little does he know that Stan Mflxnys is from the planet Pan. Read chapter 1, "Nerd Alert." Devin and his mother go to the airport and find Stan sliding down the luggage carousel. Continue reading chapter 3, "Eighty-Five Thousand Light-Years." Devin introduces Stan to his friends and classmates. Stan informs everyone that inhabitants from Pan are known as Pants. The chapter ends with Devin looking on in horror while Stan has his finger up his nose. Tantalize the audience by informing them that the reason Stan has his finger in his nostril is because he has a computer up his nose: "I've heard of laptops, but nosetops?"

Pilkey, Dav. *Ricky Ricotta's Giant Robot vs. the Voodoo Vultures from Venus*. Scholastic, 2001.

This is the third adventure about a mouse that has a giant robot for a friend. The evil vultures from Venus are tired of eating melting food and decide to take over the much cooler Earth. Read the very short chapters 1 to 9, which set up the story line and describe the vultures' attack. The evil creatures turn Ricky's teachers and classmates into mindless hypnotized victims. The last line of chapter 9 is "Ricky's Giant Robot had saved the city . . . but Victor Von Vulture had other plans."

Mix and Match Poetry

Bagert, Brod. "Spaceball." In *Giant Children*. Illustrated by Tedd Arnold. Dial, 2002.

Brown, Calef. "Moon Reunion." In *Dutch Sneakers and Flea Keepers*. Houghton Mifflin, 2000.

Dr. Seuss, "Vrooms." In *The Twentieth Century Children's Poetry Treasury*. Edited by Jack Prelutsky. Illustrated by Meilo So. Knopf, 1999.

Florian, Douglas. "My Robot." In *Bing Bang Boing*. Harcourt, 1994.

———. "UFO." In *Laugh-eteria*. Harcourt, 1999.

Holder, Julie. "The Alien." In *For Laughing Out Loud: Poems to Tickle Your Funnybone*. Edited by Jack Prelutsky. Illustrated by Marjorie Priceman. Knopf, 1991.

Hubbell, Patricia. "Message from Mars." In *The Random House Book of Poetry for Children*. Edited by Jack Prelutsky. Illustrated by Arnold Lobel. Random House, 1983.

Prelutsky, Jack. "The Creature in the Classroom." In *Kids Pick the Funniest Poems*. Edited by Bruce Lansky. Illustrated by Stephen Carpenter. Meadowbrook, 1991.

———. "An Extraterrestrial Alien." In *A Pizza the Size of the Sun*. Illustrated by James Stevenson. Greenwillow, 1996.

———. "I'm Being Abducted by Aliens" and "The Outer Space Miracle Mall." In *It's Raining Pigs and Noodles*. Illustrated by James Stevenson. Greenwillow, 2000.

Silverstein, Shel. "The Planet of Mars." In *Where the Sidewalk Ends*. HarperCollins, 1974.

Tweaking the Program Theme . . .

. . . For Preschoolers

Drop the Corey picture book and the Dadey and Jones chapter book, and substitute the following picture book:

Harper, Charise Mericle. *There Was a Bold Lady Who Wanted a Star*. Little, Brown, 2002.

> Sing the text to the tune of "There Was an Old Lady Who Swallowed a Fly." This particular bold lady wants a star, but "it seemed too far." To accomplish her goal, she buys used shoes, skates, a bike, a car, a plane, and finally a rocket. Once she catches the star, she puts it in a jar.

. . . For Fifth and Sixth Graders

Drop the Corey and Wilson picture books, and substitute the following chapter book selection:

Shusterman, Neal. *The Dark Side of Nowhere*. Little, Brown, 1997.

> Jason's boring hometown of Billington seems as if it's in the middle of nowhere. The school janitor reveals a big secret. Jason and his family are really aliens who failed in an attempt to invade Earth. The janitor gives Jason a steel glove that's a weapon. Read chapter 3, "Old Town." Begin with the sentence, "There's something I want to show you," up until the line, "'Jason,' she finally said, 'this is not normal.'" Continue with a selection from chapter 6, "Man on First." Begin with the sentence, "When I got home, all was not well," and read until the end of the chapter.

And Yet Even More Titles about Aliens Visiting Your School and Other Spacey Books for You to Consider

Best, Cari. *Shrinking Violet*. Illustrated by Giselle Potter. Farrar, Straus and Giroux, 2001.

Bradman, Tony. *It Came from Outer Space*. Illustrated by Carol Wright. Dial, 1992.

Cazet, Denys. *Minnie and Moo Save the Earth*. DK, 1999.

Cole, Babette. *Trouble with Gran*. Putnam, 1987.

Cole, Joanna. *The Magic School Bus: Lost in the Solar System*. Illustrated by Bruce Degen. Scholastic, 1990.

Duffey, Betsy. *Alien for Rent*. Delacorte, 1999.

Gilmore, Kate. *The Exchange Student*. Houghton Mifflin, 1999.

Joosse, Barbara M. *Alien Brain Fryout*. Clarion, 2000.

Karas, G. Brian. *Bebe's Bad Dream*. Greenwillow, 2000.

Mackel, Kathy. *Can of Worms*. Avon, 1999.

Pike, Christopher. *Creature in the Teacher*. Pocket, 1996.

Pinkwater, Jill. *Mister Fred*. Dutton, 1994.

Sachar, Louis. *Marvin Redpost: A Flying Birthday Cake?* Random House, 1999.

Sadler, Marilyn. *Alistair and the Alien Invasion*. Illustrated by Roger Bollen. Simon and Schuster, 1994.

SEVEN

Big and Bad
The Big Bad Wolf

Lesson Plan at a Glance

OPENING QUESTION:	Selections from *Why Do Wolves Howl? Questions and Answers about Wolves* by Melvin Berger and Gilda Berger
POEM:	"Always Be Kind to Animals" from *Big, Bad, and a Little Bit Scary: Poems That Bite Back!* by John Gardner
ORAL TALE:	*The Gunniwolf* by Wilhelmina Harper
PICTURE BOOK:	*The Three Little Wolves and the Big Bad Pig* by Eugene Trivizas
CHAPTER BOOK SELECTION:	Selections from *Little Wolf's Book of Badness* by Ian Whybrow
POEMS:	Selections from *Little Wolf's Handy Book of Poems* by Ian Whybrow
MUSICAL ACTIVITY:	"Little Rap Riding Hood" from *Crazy Gibberish and Other Story Hour Stretches (from a Storyteller's Bag of Tricks)* by Naomi Baltuck
PICTURE BOOK/CREATIVE DRAMATICS:	*Bad Boys* by Margie Palatini
PICTURE BOOK:	*The Three Pigs* by David Wiesner
DRAWING ACTIVITY:	"The Three Pigs"

Preparation and Presentation

As the audience enters the program area, play actual wolf howls from one of the many nature sound effects recordings available on the market. Since the poor wolf has been portrayed as the bad guy from early folklore throughout modern-day children's books, start this program by reading Ed Young's dedication from his Caldecott Award–winning picture book, *Lon Po Po: A Red Riding Hood Story from China* (the book citation is at the end of this chapter):

> To all the wolves in the world for lending their good name as a tangible symbol for our darkness.

OPENING QUESTION

Berger, Melvin, and Gilda Berger. *Why Do Wolves Howl? Questions and Answers about Wolves.* Scholastic, 2001.

"Why do wolves howl?" (Answer: to send messages.) Sprinkle questions from the book throughout the program. Sample questions from the book include "What is a wolf's strongest sense?" (smell); "How long can a wolf go without food?" (several days at a time); and "Do wolves make good pets?" (no). Allow the kids to react to each question and answer before moving on to your next story or activity.

POEM

Gardner, John. "Always Be Kind to Animals." In *Big, Bad, and a Little Bit Scary: Poems That Bite Back!* Edited and illustrated by Wade Zahares. Viking, 2001.

Share the large, two-page spread of wolves traveling in a nighttime winter forest that accompanies Gardner's very short, clever poem.

ORAL TALE

Harper, Wilhelmina. *The Gunniwolf.* Illustrated by Barbara Upton. Dutton, 2003.

A little girl strays into the jungle in pursuit of pretty flowers. A wolf hears her song and asks her to repeat it. The girl eventually escapes by lulling the wolf to sleep with the song. Other sources for this story can be found in the following collections:

> MacDonald, Margaret Read. *Twenty Tellable Tales.* Wilson, 1986.
>
> Sierra, Judy. *Nursery Tales around the World.* Clarion, 1996.

PICTURE BOOK

Trivizas, Eugene. *The Three Little Wolves and the Big Bad Pig.* Illustrated by Helen Oxenbury. Margaret K. McElderry, 1993.

My all-time favorite "fractured tale" shows the wolves as the good guys. Three "cuddly little wolves with soft fur and fluffy tails" go out into the world to build a house. A big bad pig knocks down their brick house with a sledgehammer, their concrete house with a pneumatic drill, and their extremely safe house (reinforced with barbed wire and metal padlocks) with dynamite. The big bad pig becomes the big good pig once he smells the fragrance of the wolves' last house, which is made of flowers.

CHAPTER BOOK SELECTION

Whybrow, Ian. *Little Wolf's Book of Badness.* Carolrhoda, 1999.

Little Wolf is sent on a journey to learn how to be a big bad wolf from Uncle Bigbad. The chapters are comprised of Little Wolf's letters to home. Read a variety of these letters as Little Wolf learns the "9 Rules of Badness." Exceptional selections include "Day 15," in which Little Wolf learns the first two rules from Uncle Bigbad's encounter with the Three Little Pigs. Be sure to share the "Day 44, Parts 1 and 2," "Day 45," and "Day 47" entries, which detail Uncle Bigbad's fatal encounter with baked beans.

The following books in Whybrow's Little Wolf series contain alternative reading selections:

Dear Little Wolf. First Avenue, 2002.

Little Wolf, Forest Detective. Carolrhoda, 2001.

Little Wolf, Pack Leader. Carolrhoda, 2003.

Little Wolf's Diary of Daring Deeds. Carolrhoda, 2000.

Little Wolf's Haunted Hall for Small Horrors. Carolrhoda, 2000.

POEMS

Whybrow, Ian. *Little Wolf's Handy Book of Poems.* First Avenue, 2002.

Sprinkle a variety of Little Wolf poems throughout the remainder of the story program, even during the upcoming drawing activity. Favorite poems include "My Bad Uncle (M.I.P.)," in which Little Wolf asks insulting questions; "Kind of an Adventure Poem, But More Muckabouty," in which audience members can act out the motions first of making and then jumping on sand pies; and "Bakebean Bangs." Read this last poem in conjunction with the above chapter selection, where Uncle Bigbad explodes from eating too many baked beans. Other fun poems from this collection include "If I Was a Teecher," and "Old MacDonald," which encourages the audience to go "E-I-E-I-arrrooo!"

MUSICAL ACTIVITY

Baltuck, Naomi. "Little Rap Riding Hood." *Crazy Gibberish and Other Story Hour Stretches (from a Storyteller's Bag of Tricks)*. Linnet, 1993.

Don a pair of sunglasses and rap out Baltuck's hip version of "Little Red Riding Hood": "Once upon a time, there lived in the woods / A boss little girl named Riding Hood . . ."

PICTURE BOOK/CREATIVE DRAMATICS

Palatini, Margie. *Bad Boys*. Illustrated by Henry Cole. HarperCollins, 2003.

Little Red Riding Hood and the Three Little Pigs send "those bad boys, Willy and Wally Wolf," on the run. The two wolves try to outsmart a group of sheep, including Meryl Sheep, by passing themselves off as the missing Bo Peep Sheep. Smart Betty Mutton says, "I know the Peep Sheep. I grazed with the Peep Sheep. . . . And you don't leap like Peep Sheep" before exposing the bad boys. This is a good source for a creative dramatic presentation or reader's theater. There are roles for the two wolves, a number of sheep, and one or two narrators.

PICTURE BOOK

Wiesner, David. *The Three Pigs*. Clarion, 2001.

Older kids will appreciate Wiesner's radical approach to this well-known folktale. The wolf blows the first pig right out of the story and into a whole new art medium and story line.

DRAWING ACTIVITY

"The Three Pigs"

Point out the different artistic styles Wiesner uses in his book *The Three Pigs*. Set out drawing materials for the children to create their own new versions of this story. Let them explore and draw the different characters in a variety of media,

such as paints, pencils, pens, crayons, chalk, and charcoal. Provide old maga-
zines to cut up and colored paper to make collage creatures. Post the completed
artwork on the library walls.

Mix and Match Picture Books

Brown, Ken. *What's the Time, Grandma Wolf?* Peachtree, 2001.

Grandma Wolf, who looks a lot like Red Riding Hood's grandmother,
answers the various forest creatures' repeated title question with humorous
replies. Brown based the story line on a game that is appropriate for a follow-
up activity to the book. The game's instructions appear at the end of the story.

Christelow, Eileen. *Where's the Big Bad Wolf?* Clarion, 2002.

Detective Doggedly tries to solve the case of the destruction of the Three
Little Pigs' homes. The wolf claims that he was too sick to have caused the
trouble. However, after he's caught fibbing, he promises, promises, promises
to "never blow another house down."

Grimm, Jacob, and Wilhelm Grimm. *Wolf and the Seven Little Kids.* Illustrated
by Anne Blades. Groundwood Books, 1999.

This is a fairly new version of the classic story of a young goat that saves the
day when the wolf gobbles down the goat's siblings.

Hartman, Bob. *The Wolf Who Cried Boy.* Illustrated by Tim Raglin. Putnam, 2002.

Little Wolf dislikes eating Lamburgers and Sloppy Does. Father Wolf remi-
nisces about eating Boy Chops and Boys-n-Berry Pie. Mother Wolf promises
to cook a boy. This is a hilarious retelling of the Aesop fable "The Boy Who
Cried Wolf."

Judes, Marie-Odile. *Max, the Stubborn Little Wolf.* Illustrated by Martine
Bourre. HarperCollins, 2001.

Max does not want to grow up to be a hunter like his father. Max would
rather be a florist.

Kimmel, Eric. *Nanny Goat and the Seven Little Kids.* Illustrated by Janet
Stevens. Holiday House, 1990.

In this humorous version of the traditional "The Wolf and the Seven Kids,"
this wolf is dressed in a T-shirt that reads "Big and Bad."

Lasky, Kathryn. *Porkenstein*. Illustrated by David Jarvis. Scholastic, 2002.

Dr. Pig, whose "two brothers were eaten by the Big Bad Wolf a year ago," creates a monstrous, gigantic pig. Of course, the Big Bad Wolf comes knocking on the door and licking his chops at the thought of such a huge dinner.

Levine, Gail Carson. *Betsy Who Cried Wolf*. Illustrated by Scott Nash. HarperCollins, 2002.

This retelling of the fable "The Boy Who Cried Wolf" features a hungry wolf "with a plan" that outwits a shepherdess. In the end, however, the wolf saves some lambs from falling off a cliff. There are plenty of opportunities for the audience to howl like a wolf (and to howl with laughter).

Whatley, Bruce. *Wait! No Paint!* HarperCollins, 2001.

Three Little Pigs meet both the Big Bad Wolf and the illustrator of the book. This book has great lines for reading aloud. For example, the wolf hollers, "Yemt me yin, yemt me yin . . . or I'll yuff and I'll nuff . . ." after his nose gets smacked by a door. The illustrator kindly redraws the wolf's nose.

Mix and Match Chapter Book Selection

Bauer, Marion Dane. *Runt*. Clarion, 2002.

Runt is a small wolf that tries to prove his worth to the rest of the pack. Read either chapter 1, when we first meet Runt, or chapter 8, when Runt encounters a nasty porcupine.

Mix and Match Oral Tales

Shannon, George. *A Knock at the Door*. Oryx, 1992.

This anthology contains several variants of the traditional "The Wolf and the Seven Kids" story ready for oral telling.

Sierra, Judy. "Big Pig, Little Pig, Speckled Pig, and Runt." In *Can You Guess My Name? Traditional Tales around the World*. Clarion, 2002.

This is a fun African American version of the Three Little Pigs story ("Mama sow knew she was going to kick the bucket . . .").

Sierra, Judy. "Groundhog's Dance." In *Nursery Tales around the World.* Clarion, 1996.

> A trapped groundhog outwits seven wolves by teaching them a dance. Teach your audience the groundhog's song: "Ha wi ye-a hi / Ya ha wi ye-a hi." This story also explains why the groundhog has a short tail.

Mix and Match Creative Dramatics

Sierra, Judy. "The Wolf, the Goat, and the Cabbage." In *Multicultural Folktales for the Feltboard and Reader's Theater.* Oryx, 1996.

> This riddle story cleverly shows how a man can transport a wolf, a goat, and a basket of cabbage one at a time across a river in a boat without the wolf eating the goat and the goat eating the cabbage. Sierra sets up the story as a felt-board story or to read as a very short reader's theater activity.

Wolf, J. M. *Cinderella Outgrows the Glass Slipper and Other Zany Fractured Fairy Tale Plays.* Scholastic Professional Books, 2002.

> The wolf is the good character in this retelling of "Little Red Riding Hood."

Mix and Match Poetry

Esbensen, Barbara Juster. "Wolf." In *The Twentieth Century Children's Poetry Treasury.* Edited by Jack Prelutsky. Illustrated by Meilo So. Knopf, 1999.

Florian, Douglas. "The Wolf." In *Bow Wow Meow Meow: It's Rhyming Cats and Dogs.* Harcourt, 2003.

Hughes, Ted. "Wolf." In *Beauty of the Beast: Poems from the Animal Kingdom.* Edited by Jack Prelutsky. Illustrated by Meilo So. Knopf, 1997.

Nicholls, Judith. "Wolf." In *Beauty of the Beast: Poems from the Animal Kingdom.* Edited by Jack Prelutsky. Illustrated by Meilo So. Knopf, 1997.

Prelutsky, Jack. "A Wolf Is at the Laundromat." In *The New Kid on the Block.* Illustrated by James Stevenson. Greenwillow, 1984.

Sargent, William D. "Wind—Wolves." In *The Random House Book of Poetry for Children.* Edited by Jack Prelutsky. Illustrated by Arnold Lobel. Random House, 1983.

Wheeler, Lisa. "Harry." In *Wool Gathering: A Sheep Family Reunion.* Illustrated by Frank Ansley. Atheneum, 2001.

Tweaking the Program Theme . . .

. . . For Preschoolers

Drop the Palatini dramatic activity and the drawing activity, and substitute any picture book from the "Mix and Match Picture Book" section plus the following title:

Puttock, Simon. *Big Bad Wolf Is Good.* Illustrated by Lynne Chapman. Sterling, 2002.

> Big Bad Wolf tries to convince others that he is not so bad. The reactions from Mrs. Goose and her goslings are hilarious. They make faces at the wolf through their windows. The kids in the audience can also make funny faces at the wolf.

. . . For Fifth and Sixth Graders

Drop the Harper oral tale, and substitute the following chapter book selection:

Paulsen, Gary. *Woodsong.* Bradbury, 1990.

> Read the episode in chapter 4, where Paulsen saves a doe from a pack of wolves. Begin with the line, "We had run long in a day . . ." and read until the sentence, "I would have thought it all a dream except that her tracks and the tracks of the wolves were there in the morning." There is another section of the book in which Paulsen tells of a doe killed by wolves, but it is fairly graphic for a library story program setting.

And Yet Even More Titles Featuring the Big Bad Wolf (and Some Nice Wolves) for You to Consider

Ada, Alma Flor. *Yours Truly, Goldilocks.* Illustrated by Leslie Tryon. Atheneum, 1998.

Bloom, Becky. *Wolf!* Illustrated by Pascal Biet. Orchard, 1999.

Blundell, Tony. *Beware of Boys.* Greenwillow, 1992.

Brandenburg, Jim. *Scruffy: A Wolf Finds His Place in the Pack.* Walker, 1996.

Child, Lauren. *Beware of the Storybook Wolves.* Scholastic, 2000.

Denslow, Sharon Phillips. *Big Wolf and Little Wolf.* Illustrated by Cathie Felstead. Greenwillow, 2000.

Ernst, Lisa Campbell. *Little Red Riding Hood: A Newfangled Prairie Tale.* Simon and Schuster, 1995.

Fearnley, Jan. *Mr. Wolf and the Three Bears*. Harcourt, 2002.

———. *Mr. Wolf's Pancakes*. Little Tiger, 1999.

George, Jean Craighead. *Look to the North: A Wolf Pup Diary*. Illustrated by Lucia Washburn. HarperCollins, 1997.

Hobbs, Will. *Howling Hill*. Illustrated by Jill Kastner. Morrow, 1998.

Kasza, Keiko. *The Wolf's Chicken Stew*. Putnam, 1987.

Kimmel, Eric. *Sirko and the Wolf*. Illustrated by Robert Sauber. Holiday House, 1997.

Kitamura, Satoshi. *Sheep in Wolves' Clothing*. Farrar, Straus and Giroux, 1995.

London, Jonathan. *The Eyes of Gray Wolf*. Illustrated by Jon Van Zyle. Chronicle, 1993.

MacDonald, Elizabeth. *The Wolf Is Coming!* Illustrated by Ken Brown. Dutton, 1998.

Masurel, Claire. *Big Bad Wolf*. Illustrated by Melissa Iwai. Scholastic, 2002.

Meddaugh, Susan. *The Best Place*. Houghton, 1999.

———. *Hog-Eye*. Houghton, 1995.

Murphy, Jim. *The Call of the Wolves*. Illustrated by Mark Alan Weatherby. Scholastic, 1989.

Novak, Matt. *Little Wolf, Big Wolf*. HarperCollins, 2000.

Numeroff, Laura Joffe. *The Chicken Sisters*. Illustrated by Sharleen Collicott. HarperCollins, 1997.

Pinkwater, Daniel. *Wolf Christmas*. Illustrated by Jill Pinkwater. Marshall Cavendish, 1998.

Puttock, Simon. *Big Bad Wolf Is Good*. Sterling, 2002.

Scieszka, Jon. *The True Story of the Three Little Pigs*. Illustrated by Lane Smith. Viking, 1989.

Young, Ed. *Lon Po Po: A Red Riding Hood Story from China*. Philomel, 1989.

EIGHT

Big and Bad
Fox and Coyote

Lesson Plan at a Glance

PICTURE BOOK:	*The Tale of Tricky Fox* by Jim Aylesworth
CHAPTER BOOK SELECTION:	*Ereth's Birthday* by Avi
PICTURE BOOK:	*Kissing Coyotes* by Marcia Vaughan
ORAL TALE:	"Rabbit and Fox" from *The Boy Who Lived with the Bears* by Joseph Bruchac
PICTURE BOOK:	*My Lucky Day* by Keiko Kasza
ORAL TALE:	"Brer Wolf Tries to Catch Brer Rabbit" from *The Tales of Uncle Remus: The Adventures of Brer Rabbit* by Julius Lester
POEM:	"The Coyote" from *Mammalabilia* by Douglas Florian
READER'S THEATER:	"The Tricks of a Fox" from *Multicultural Folktales for the Feltboard and Reader's Theater* by Judy Sierra
ACTIVITY:	Storytelling Circle Swaps

Preparation and Presentation

Fox and Coyote, and sometimes their canine cousins Hyena and Dingo, are usually cunning and tricky "bad guys." Some of the stories demonstrate their cunning.

Most of the stories, however, feature these tricksters being "outfoxed" by smaller characters. Start the show off with a group coyote howl. Aarrooo!

PICTURE BOOK

Aylesworth, Jim. *The Tale of Tricky Fox.* Illustrated by Barbara McClintock. Scholastic, 2001.

> Tricky Fox fools a series of humans in order to eat a pig. After each trick, Fox sings, "I'm so clever / tee-hee-hee / Trick, trick, tricky / Yes, siree." Have the kids join this boastful chant. In the end, we learn that the fox was unable to fool someone—a teacher!

CHAPTER BOOK SELECTION

Avi. *Ereth's Birthday.* HarperCollins, 2000.

> Ereth, the porcupine from Avi's Poppy series, promises a dying fox mother that he'll take care of her pups. Read chapter 15, "Chores." Ereth tries to bring order to the fox den but quickly loses his patience. Here's a delightful sample of Ereth's angry command of the language: "'Moose midges on frog fudge!' Ereth barked."

PICTURE BOOK

Vaughan, Marcia. *Kissing Coyotes.* Illustrated by Kenneth J. Spengler. Rising Moon, 2002.

> Jack Rabbit brags that he can do-si-do with a rattlesnake, scare off a herd of longhorns, skedaddle past a skunk yelling "Woo, woo, stinky-poo!" and kiss a he-coyote, a she-coyote, and a wee coyote. The tall tale–type language is fun to read aloud. Although this is a good choice for learning as an oral tale, you'll want to be sure to share Spengler's sharp, close-up illustrations of the wacky characters.

ORAL TALE

Bruchac, Joseph. "Rabbit and Fox." In *The Boy Who Lived with the Bears.* Illustrated by Murv Jacob. HarperCollins, 1995.

> Fox follows Rabbit's tracks in the snow. Rabbit then disguises himself as an old woman and an old man.

PICTURE BOOK

Kasza, Keiko. *My Lucky Day.* Putnam, 2003.

> A pig "mistakenly" shows up at a fox's door. We find out later that the pig's "mistake" was really part of a very clever plan. Once in the house, the pig tricks the fox into preparing a bath, cooking a nice dinner, and giving a massage. Try telling the two-character story with hand puppets.

ORAL TALE

Lester, Julius. "Brer Wolf Tries to Catch Brer Rabbit." In *The Tales of Uncle Remus: The Adventures of Brer Rabbit.* Illustrated by Jerry Pinkney. Dial, 1987.

> This very short tale is one of my all-time favorite Brer Rabbit adaptations. Brer Wolf and Brer Fox try to trick Brer Rabbit into believing that Brer Fox has passed away. They attempt to lure Brer Rabbit into their house and pounce on him. Brer Rabbit hilariously tricks Brer Fox into revealing that he isn't really dead. Brer Rabbit announces that he always heard that dead folks raise their legs and holler "Wahoo!" Brer Fox then raises his leg and hollers "Wahoo!"

POEM

Florian, Douglas. "The Coyote." In *Mammalabilia.* Harcourt, 2000.

> Florian manages to fit a coyote howl into the text of this short poem. Have the audience give, yet again, one more group coyote howl.

READER'S THEATER

Sierra, Judy. "The Tricks of a Fox." In *Multicultural Folktales for the Feltboard and Reader's Theater.* Oryx, 1996.

> Fox's cunning comes full circle as he outwits the creatures of the sea after being trapped on a tiny island by Eagle. The story can be told orally, as a felt-board production (the book comes with patterns), or as a reader's theater production.

ACTIVITY

Storytelling Circle Swaps

> Since Fox and Coyote figure so prominently in Native American and African American folklore, involving the audience in storytelling activities and games is a nice tie-in to the featured stories. Some of the following storytelling games were inspired from the following resource:

Livo, Norma J., and Sandra A. Rietz. *Storytelling Activities*. Libraries Unlimited, 1987.

This is a common storytelling activity. Have the audience sit in a circle. Someone starts a story, stops at a certain point and says to the next person, "and then what happened?" That person adds another thread to the story and passes it on to the next person, and so on until the story has traveled the entire circle.

Another version is to allow everyone to tell his or her own complete short story. Give them a "jump-start phrase" to allow them to focus on a specific story thread. Examples include, "I have a pet, and the silliest thing it ever did was . . ." (You can substitute *pet* with *brother, sister, mother, father, friend*, etc.); "My most embarrassing moment was . . ."; or "Let me tell you what happened to me yesterday when . . ."

Mix and Match Picture Books

Kellogg, Steven. *Chicken Little*. Morrow, 1985.

Foxy Loxy has visions of poultry meals in his head. He disguises himself as Officer Loxy to investigate why the sky is falling on Chicken Little's head.

Leeson, Christine. *Clever Little Freddy*. Illustrated by Joanne Moss. Little Tiger, 1997.

This is a funny little story of a young fox that sneaks human food instead of catching natural prey.

Lowell, Susan. *The Three Little Javelinas*. Illustrated by Jim Harris. Northland, 1992.

This retelling of "The Three Little Pigs" is set in the American Southwest and features three peccaries, or wild pigs. Coyote blows down the houses made of tumbleweed and saguaro sticks. The third pig makes his house with strong adobe. When Coyote falls in the woodstove, he lets loose with a "Yip, yap, yeep, YEE-OWW-OOOOOOOOOOOOOOO!"

Lund, Jillian. *Two Cool Coyotes*. Dutton, 1999.

Frank and Angelina "were two coyotes living in a hot American desert." They practice their howling and wear sunglasses and bandannas (Angelina's bandanna has smiley faces). Then Angelina moves away. If you have a coyote puppet, dress it up with sunglasses and a bandanna. If you don't have a puppet, then wear the sunglasses and bandanna yourself.

McDermott, Gerald. *Coyote: A Trickster Tale from the American Southwest.* Harcourt, 1994.

Foolish Coyote tries to fly with the crows. Because of his vanity and demands, he falls from the sky. His beautiful blue fur turns to the color of dust.

McKissack, Patricia. *Flossie and the Fox.* Illustrated by Rachel Isadora. Dial, 1986.

Lil' Flossie has never seen a fox before. She demands proof of the creature in front of her that he really is a fox. In the end, Flossie outfoxes the fox.

Sierra, Judy. *Mean Hyena: A Folktale from Malawi.* Illustrated by Michael Bryant. Dutton, 1997.

Clever tortoise gets revenge after hyena traps him in the crook of a tree. This trickster *pourquoi* story tells how hyena got both his laugh and his dirty, ugly coat.

Stevens, Janet. *Coyote Steals the Blanket.* Holiday House, 1993.

Coyote ignores Hummingbird's warning and steals some beautiful blankets that belong to the spirit of the great desert. The spirit sends a "killer rock" after Coyote.

Ward, Helen. *The Rooster and the Fox.* Millbrook, 2003.

This is a gorgeous picture book adaptation of a Chaucer tale that is just right for the school-age group. Mr. Fox steals off with the vain rooster Chanticleer. Share the chart of rare farm breeds found in the book's back matter.

Mix and Match Oral Tales

Bruchac, Joseph. "Why Coyote Has Yellow Eyes." In *Native American Animal Stories.* Fulcrum, 1992.

This story is similar to MacDonald's story "Coyote's Crying Song," listed below.

MacDonald, Margaret Read. "Coyote's Crying Song." In *Twenty Tellable Tales.* Wilson, 1986.

Coyote wants to learn Little Dove's song and threatens to eat her if she doesn't teach him.

Sierra, Judy. "The Coyote and the Rabbit." In *Nursery Tales around the World*. Illustrated by Stefano Vitale. Clarion, 1996.

 With the help of his relatives, Rabbit tricks Coyote into thinking that creatures with short tails are faster than those with long tails.

Sierra, Judy. "The Fox and the Crab." In *Nursery Tales around the World*. Illustrated by Stefano Vitale. Clarion, 1996.

 This is a short fable from China. Crab hangs on to Fox's bushy tail and convinces Fox that crabs are faster runners.

Mix and Match Poetry

Chandra, Deborah. "Fox." In *Beauty of the Beast: Poems from the Animal Kingdom*. Edited by Jack Prelutsky. Illustrated by Meilo So. Knopf, 1997.

Hoberman, Mary Ann. "Foxes." In *The Llama Who Had No Pajama: 100 Favorite Poems*. Illustrated by Betty Fraser. Harcourt, 1998; and in *Sing a Song of Popcorn*. Edited by Beatrice Schenk de Regniers. Scholastic, 1988.

Hubbell, Patricia. "The Spun Gold Fox." In *Beauty of the Beast: Poems from the Animal Kingdom*. Edited by Jack Prelutsky. Illustrated by Meilo So. Knopf, 1997.

Ipcar, Dahlov. "Red Fox at Dawn." In *Beauty of the Beast: Poems from the Animal Kingdom*. Edited by Jack Prelutsky. Illustrated by Meilo So. Knopf, 1997.

Singer, Marilyn. "Red Fox." In *Fireflies at Midnight*. Illustrated by Ken Robbins. Atheneum, 2003.

Volborth, Judith Mountain-Leaf. "Coyote Blue." In *Knock at a Star*. Rev. ed. Edited by X. J. Kennedy and Dorothy M. Kennedy. Illustrated by Karen Lee Baker. Little, Brown, 1999.

Tweaking the Program Theme . . .

. . . For Preschoolers

Use the felt-board version of the Sierra story. Drop the Avi chapter book selection and the Bruchac oral tale, and substitute the following picture books:

Crum, Shutta. *Fox and Fluff*. Illustrated by John Bendall-Brunello. Whitman, 2002.

Fox is smitten with a little chick that does its best to act tough. The chick's constant peeps punctuate the humor of the story, climaxing in a "GrrrPeep!" This picture book also makes a good reader's theater production for older kids.

Fox, Mem. *Hattie and the Fox.* Illustrated by Patricia Mullins. Macmillan, 1986.

A hen sees a nose in the bushes, then two eyes, two ears, two legs, and finally, the body of a fox. It's fun to read the various reactions and attitudes of the other farm animals.

. . . For Fifth and Sixth Graders

Drop the Aylesworth and Kasza picture books, and add another oral tale and poem from the "Mix and Match" sections. You can also expand the storytelling activities, or let the kids work on a reader's theater production for the Sierra story "The Tricks of a Fox" or the Crum picture book, *Fox and Fluff,* to present to younger children at a future program.

And Yet Even More Titles about Foxes, Coyotes, Hyenas, Dingoes, and Similar Critters for You to Consider

Aardema, Verna. *Borreguita and the Coyote: A Tale from Ayutla, Mexico.* Illustrated by Petra Mathers. Knopf, 1991.

Begay, Shonto. *Ma'ii and Cousin Horned Toad: A Traditional Navajo Story.* Scholastic, 1992.

Byars, Betsy. *The Midnight Fox.* Viking, 1968.

Campoy, F. Isabel. *Rosa Raposa.* Illustrated by Jose Aruego and Ariane Dewey. Gulliver, 2002.

Goble, Paul. *Iktomi and the Ducks: A Plains Indian Story.* Orchard, 1990.

Marshall, James. *Wings: A Tale of Two Chickens.* Houghton Mifflin, 1986.

McAllister, Angela. *Barkus, Sly, and the Golden Egg.* Illustrated by Sally Anne Lambert. Bloomsbury, 2002.

Mwenye Hadithi. *Hungry Hyena.* Illustrated by Adrienne Kennaway. Little, Brown, 1994.

Shannon, George. *Dance Away.* Illustrated by Jose Aruego and Ariane Dewey. Greenwillow, 1982.

Steig, William. *Doctor De Soto*. Farrar, Straus and Giroux, 1982.

Stevens, Janet. *Old Bag of Bones*. Holiday House, 1996.

Thomas, Jane Resh. *Fox in a Trap*. Clarion, 1987.

Vaughan, Marcia K. *Wombat Stew*. Illustrated by Pamela Lofts. Silver Burdett, 1986.

Wyllie, Stephen. *A Flea in the Ear*. Dutton, 1995.

NINE

Big and Bad
Lions and Tigers and Crocs (Oh My!)

Lesson Plan at a Glance

PICTURE BOOK:	*The Enormous Crocodile* by Roald Dahl
POEM:	"The Crocodile and the Alligator" from *Lizards, Frogs, and Polliwogs* by Douglas Florian
PICTURE BOOK/ORAL TALE:	*Mrs. Chicken and the Hungry Crocodile* by Won-Ldy Paye and Margaret H. Lippert
ORAL TALE:	"Lion's Advisors" from *Still More Stories to Solve: Fourteen Folktales from around the World* by George Shannon
PICTURE BOOK:	*Big Squeak, Little Squeak* by Robert Kraus
POEM:	"Two Mice" from *You Read to Me, I'll Read to You* by Mary Ann Hoberman
CHAPTER BOOK SELECTION:	*Class Pets: Battle in a Bottle* by Frank Asch
PICTURE BOOK/ORAL TALE:	*Subira Subira* by Tololwa M. Mollel
ACTIVITY:	Face Painting

Preparation and Presentation

Big and small cats, alligators, and crocodiles—all hungry predators looking for smaller prey to eat—continue the Big and Bad series of programs.

PICTURE BOOK

Dahl, Roald. *The Enormous Crocodile.* Illustrated by Quentin Blake. Knopf, 1978.

This long but fun read-aloud is in the spirit of a Rudyard Kipling animal story. The Enormous Crocodile sets out in search of fat, juicy children to eat. He disguises himself as a coconut tree, a seesaw, a merry-go-round ride, and a park bench. His evil plans are thwarted by Humpy-Rumpy the Hippopotamus, Trunky the Elephant, Muggle-Wump the Monkey, and the Roly-Poly Bird.

POEM

Florian, Douglas. "The Crocodile and the Alligator." In *Lizards, Frogs, and Polliwogs.* Harcourt, 2001.

The differences between the two species are explained in this short, humorous poem. Alligators are the ones that swallow second graders!

PICTURE BOOK/ORAL TALE

Paye, Won-Ldy, and Margaret H. Lippert. *Mrs. Chicken and the Hungry Crocodile.* Illustrated by Julie Paschkis. Holt, 2003.

A chicken outwits a crocodile by convincing the larger beast that the two are sisters in this traditional African story. Either read the picture book or tell it orally using puppets and plastic Easter eggs filled with cloth and replica baby chickens and baby crocs (such as cotton balls and clothespins).

ORAL TALE

Shannon, George. "Lion's Advisors." In *Still More Stories to Solve: Fourteen Folktales from around the World.* Illustrated by Peter Sís. Greenwillow, 1994.

Lion's wife tells him that he has bad breath, and that puts him in a foul mood. Lion asks Sheep if this is true. When Sheep responds that Lion's breath is indeed bad, Lion eats him. Lion next asks Wolf. Wolf says no and is eaten anyway because Lion thinks that Wolf is lying to save his skin. Lion then asks Fox. The reply Fox gives Lion both satisfies Lion and makes him sympathetic toward Fox. Ask the audience what they think Fox told Lion. The answer is, "As Fox pretended to cough, he told Lion, 'I have such a terrible cold, I can't smell anything.'"

PICTURE BOOK

Kraus, Robert. *Big Squeak, Little Squeak*. Illustrated by Kevin O'Malley. Orchard, 1996.

> Little Squeak realizes that there's more to life than eating cheese curls and watching mouse cartoons. Big Squeak and Little Squeak go into Mr. Kit Kat's cheese shop, where "many mice had gone into his store, but none had ever come out." Big Squeak outwits the cat and saves the mice trapped in the basement.

POEM

Hoberman, Mary Ann. "Two Mice." In *You Read to Me, I'll Read to You*. Illustrated by Michael Emberley. Little, Brown, 2001.

> Two cats catch two mice. Kids from the audience can read the two voices that are scripted out, or the storyteller can read one voice, with a volunteer reading the other. Feel free to continue with the following poem, "The Big Cat," in which two tough-looking dogs rescue the mice.

CHAPTER BOOK SELECTION

Asch, Frank. *Class Pets: Battle in a Bottle*. Simon and Schuster, 2003.

> Show the cool cover shot of Big Gray the cat menacing Jake the mouse. Jake is seeking refuge in an empty ketchup bottle. Read chapter 9, which describes this particular scene. Jake momentarily escapes Big Gray by tickling him with a feather, causing the cat to sneeze and shoot Jake "across the playground like a bullet." The chapter ends with Big Gray knocking Jake and the ketchup bottle toward a big drop-off. Resume the action by reading chapter 11. The two continue their battle with plenty of insults hurled back and forth.

PICTURE BOOK/ORAL TALE

Mollel, Tololwa M. *Subira Subira*. Illustrated by Linda Saport. Clarion, 2000.

> Maulidi refuses to listen to his older sister Tatu in this story based on an African folktale. The little boy throws rocks and starts fights with Tatu. The girl heads to the forest to seek the advice of MaMzuka, the spirit woman. MaMzuka gives Tatu the task of plucking three whiskers from a lion. Tatu finds the lion and sings, "Subira, subira subira, subira / Subira nijongee, subira / Nduli tafadhali, subira / Subira, subira subira, subira." Tatu applies

the lesson she learns from her task to managing her brother. The author includes a musical score and translation to the Swahili song in the book's back matter. "Subira" means patience or a call to be understood, tolerant, or calm. Teach the song to the audience before telling or reading the story.

ACTIVITY

Face Painting

Many face-painting books designed for children have patterns for creating big cat faces, à la the Broadway musical *Cats*, and other animal designs. Purchase the proper face-painting supplies, warn the parents ahead of time, line up plenty of volunteers, and check out the following resources:

Andrich, Tom. *Decorate Yourself: Cool Designs for Temporary Tattoos, Face Painting, Henna, and More.* Sterling, 2003.

Caudron, Chris, and Caro Childs. *The Usborne Book of Face Painting.* Usborne, 2003.

Face Painting Book (with Paints). Klutz, 1990.

Silver, Patricia. *Face Painting.* Kids Can, 2000.

Smith, Thomasina. *Face Painting.* Southwater, 2002.

Watt, Fiona, and Caro Childs. *Starting Face Painting.* EDC Publications, 1998.

Mix and Match Picture Books

Artell, Mike. *Petite Rouge: A Cajun Red Riding Hood.* Illustrated by Jim Harris. Dial, 2001.

This retelling is told in Cajun verse. The title character is a duck that is threatened by a mean "ol' gator." Have fun reading the tricky text with such phrases as taking a basket of "gumbo an' t'ree or two sweater" to Grand-mere.

Han, Suzanne Crowder. *The Rabbit's Tail: A Story from Korea.* Illustrated by Richard Wehrman. Holt, 1999.

A tiger fears the dried persimmon, thinking it's a powerful spirit instead of a food item. The tiger crosses paths with a thief and a rabbit, causing even more confusion. The thief finds himself riding the tiger's back while the tiger fears that the dried persimmon has hold of him. The rabbit tries to convince the tiger that the dried persimmon is really a man but loses his tail in the process. Confused? The kids won't have trouble following this rollicking, absurd folktale.

Kasza, Keiko. *The Mightiest*. Putnam, 2001.

Lion, Bear, and Elephant find a crown that they think should go to The Mightiest. They argue that each one is The Mightiest. The three decide whoever scares an old lady the most will win the crown. The old woman, in turn, saves the animals from a giant (her son). They try to give her the crown, but she turns it down.

Lester, Julius. *Sam and the Tigers*. Illustrated by Jerry Pinkney. Dial, 1996.

This respectful retelling of "Little Black Sambo" features Sam, who lives in Sam-sam-sa-mara, "where the animals and people lived and worked together like they didn't know they weren't supposed to." Sam outwits some tigers that plan to eat him. This is yet another marvelous read-aloud that is pure pleasure for the tongue.

MacDonald, Margaret Read. *Mabela the Clever*. Illustrated by Tim Coffey. Albert Whitman, 2001.

In the early times, when mice were foolish, they were easy prey for the clever Cat. One mouse, Mabela, learns about cleverness herself. This advice comes in handy when Cat leads a group of mice on a dangerous march. MacDonald includes advice for audience participation and a tune to play for an active Mabela game.

Soto, Gary. *Chato's Kitchen*. Illustrated by Susan Guevara. Putnam, 1995.

Chato the cat notices a "whole family of fat, juicy mice moving into the house next door." He invites the mice over for dinner, all the while planning to make them the main course, "chorizo con mice."

Xiong, Blia. *Nine-in-One Grr! Grr!* Adapted by Cathy Spagnoli. Illustrated by Nancy Hom. Children's Book Press, 1989.

This Hmong folktale explains why there are so few "tigers on the earth today." The great god Shao tells Tiger that she will have nine cubs each year as long as she remembers his words. Tiger goes around reminding herself by chanting, "Nine-in-one, Grr! Grr!" Bird is worried that too many tiger cubs will eat up all the birds. Bird tricks Tiger into chanting, "One-in-nine, Grr! Grr! . . . one cub every nine years."

Mix and Match Chapter Book Selections

Avi. *Ragweed.* Avon, 1999.

Ragweed is a country mouse headed to the city on a train in this prequel to Avi's book *Poppy.* Read chapter 3, "Silversides." We meet Silversides, a white cat who hates mice so much that she forms F.E.A.R., which stands for Felines Enraged About Rodents. "The only good mouse is a dead mouse." Continue reading chapter 4, "To the City." Ragweed arrives only to run into Silversides. The chapter ends with the line, "the cat was preparing her deadly pounce."

King-Smith, Dick. *Martin's Mice.* Crown, 1989.

Martin is a farm cat who dislikes eating mice. Read chapter 1. Dulce Maude, Martin's mother, brings her children mice to "worry" and eat. She then tells them to learn to hunt for themselves. Martin roams the farm and learns the concept of owning a pet. He catches a frightened mouse. She tells him to hurry and be done killing her. "'Not on your life!' said Martin. 'I'm going to keep you for a pet!'"

Mix and Match Short Story Selections

Kipling, Rudyard. "The Beginning of the Armadillos." In *Just So Stories.* Illustrated by Barry Moser. Morrow, 1996.

A young Painted Jaguar tries to eat the Stickly-Prickly Hedgehog and the Slow-and-Solid Tortoise. The two fool the young feline during their first encounter but worry that they won't be able to trick him again. Hedgehog and Tortoise swap parts and evolve into a new creature that Mother Jaguar names Armadillo.

Marshall, James. *Rats on the Range and Other Stories.* Dial, 1993.

Read the first short story, "Miss Mouse," in this humorous collection. A mouse mistakenly arrives at the wrong house in answer to an ad for a housekeeper. Thomas J. Cat is delighted to have a mouse arrive at his door and plans to eat her as soon as she's done cleaning. He eventually grows fond of her. To her horror, she finds a recipe for "Mouse Mousse" and flees. The cat misses her, but upon her return, he is delighted to sign a legal document forswearing mouse meat.

Mix and Match Oral Tales

Aesop. "Androcles and the Lion." In *Aesop's Fables*. Illustrated by Jerry Pinkney. SeaStar, 2000.

Androcles is a slave who manages to run away from his cruel master. He finds a lion that is in pain from a sharp thorn buried in its paw. Androcles helps the grateful lion. Both are captured. Androcles is thrown into an arena to be torn apart by a lion. The lion turns out to be the one he befriended. When the emperor sees the lion crouch at Androcles' feet, he pardons "this slave who can tame lions."

Sierra, Judy. "The Rabbit and the Tiger: A Vietnamese Folktale." In *Multicultural Folktales for the Feltboard and Reader's Theater*. Oryx, 1996.

Rabbit outwits Tiger three ways: by tricking Tiger into eating red-hot chilies, by banging a wasp's nest (the tiger thinks it's a drum), and by wearing a snake as a belt. This is a good story to tell aloud in addition to performing it with felt characters or as a reader's theater.

Mix and Match Poetry

Dahl, Roald. "The Crocodile" and "The Lion." In *Dirty Beasts*. Rev. ed. Illustrated by Quentin Blake. Puffin, 1986.

Esbensen, Barbara. "Lion." In *Beauty of the Beast: Poems from the Animal Kingdom*. Edited by Jack Prelutsky. Illustrated by Meilo So. Knopf, 1997.

Flanders, Michael. "The Crocodile." In *The Twentieth Century Children's Poetry Treasury*. Edited by Jack Prelutsky. Illustrated by Meilo So. Knopf, 1999; and in *Beauty of the Beast: Poems from the Animal Kingdom*. Edited by Jack Prelutsky. Illustrated by Meilo So. Knopf, 1997.

Florian, Douglas. "The Black Panther," "The Cheetah," "The Jaguarundi," "The Leopard," "The Lion," and "The Ocelot." In *Bow Wow Meow Meow: It's Rhyming Cats and Dogs*. Harcourt, 2003.

Herford, Oliver. "The Cantankerous 'Gator." In *Never Take a Pig to Lunch and Other Poems about the Fun of Eating*. Edited and illustrated by Nadine Bernard Westcott. Orchard, 1994.

Hoberman, Mary Ann. "Alligator/Crocodile." In *The Llama Who Had No Pajama*. Illustrated by Betty Fraser. Harcourt, 1998.

Kennedy, X. J. "Crocodile." In *Exploding Gravy: Poems to Make You Laugh*. Illustrated by Joy Allen. Little, Brown, 2002.

Kuskin, Karla. "There Was a Mouse." In *Moon, Have You Met My Mother?* Illustrated by Sergio Ruzzier. Laura Geringer, 2003.

Lansky, Bruce. "Mrs. Doodle." In *A Bad Case of the Giggles*. Illustrated by Stephen Carpenter. Meadowbrook, 1994.

MacDonald, Mary. "The Alligators." In *For Laughing Out Loud: Poems to Tickle Your Funnybone*. Edited by Jack Prelutsky. Illustrated by Marjorie Priceman. Knopf, 1991.

Merrian, Eve. "Alligator on the Escalator." In *Tomie DePaola's Book of Poems*. Edited and illustrated by Tomie DePaola. Putnam, 1988.

Prelutsky, Jack. "Alligators Are Unfriendly." In *The New Kid on the Block*. Illustrated by James Stevenson. Greenwillow, 1984.

———. "We're Four Ferocious Tigers." In *Something Big Has Been Here*. Illustrated by James Stevenson. Greenwillow, 1990.

Schertle, Alice. "Cheetah: The Race." In *Advice for a Frog*. Illustrated by Norman Green. Lothrop, Lee and Shepard, 1995.

Silverstein, Shel. "Feeding Time." In *Falling Up*. HarperCollins, 1996.

Tiller, Ruth. "The Hunter." In *The Twentieth Century Children's Poetry Treasury*. Edited by Jack Prelutsky. Illustrated by Meilo So. Knopf, 1999.

Tweaking the Program Theme . . .

. . . For Preschoolers

Drop the Dahl and Mollel picture books, and substitute the following picture books:

Dr. Seuss. *I Can Lick Thirty Tigers Today*. Random House, 1969.

A funny small Cat in the Hat brags about fighting thirty tigers. When thirty tigers actually show up, the cat dismisses most of them for several reasons (their fingernails are dirty, they need a nap, etc.). He finally tells the final tiger that he'll beat him up "right after lunch."

Hoberman, Mary Ann. *It's Simple, Said Simon*. Illustrated by Meilo So. Knopf, 2001.

Simon imitates a dog's growl, a cat's stretch, and a horse's jump. He uses all three skills to impress a tiger. When the tiger tricks Simon into jumping on its back and then tells the boy that he is going to eat him, Simon cleverly escapes in the river. The audience can growl, stretch, and jump along with Simon.

. . . For Fifth and Sixth Graders

Drop the Kraus and Paye picture books, and substitute the following chapter book selection:

Taylor, Theodore. *Lord of the Kill*. Scholastic, 2002.

The Los Coyotes Preserve is a big cat compound, home to lions, tigers, cheetahs, leopards, jaguars, and cougars that are discards from circuses and private owners. Read chapter 2, "General Dmitri Zukov." Ben finds that the big cats are acting strangely. Continue with chapter 3, "The Bloody Jaguars." Ben finds the jaguars covered in blood with a human corpse in their cage.

And Yet Even More Titles about Big and Bad Felines and Reptiles for You to Consider

Axtell, David. *We're Going on a Lion Hunt*. Holt, 1999.

Baumgartner, Barbara. *Crocodile! Crocodile! Stories Told around the World*. Illustrated by Judith Moffatt. DK, 1994.

Bloom, Becky. *Crackers*. Illustrated by Pascal Biet. Orchard, 2001.

Bryan, Ashley. *Lion and the Ostrich Chicks and Other African Folk Tales*. Atheneum, 1986.

Campoy, F. Isabel. *Rosa Raposa*. Illustrated by Jose Aruego and Ariane Dewey. Harcourt, 2002.

Day, Nancy Raines. *The Lion's Whiskers: An Ethiopian Folktale*. Illustrated by Ann Grifalconi. Scholastic, 1995.

Diakite, Baba Wague. *The Hunterman and the Crocodile*. Scholastic, 1997.

Duncan, Lois. *Song of the Circus*. Illustrated by Meg Cundif. Philomel, 2002.

Emberley, Michael. *Ruby.* Little, Brown, 1990.

Kasza, Keiko. *The Rat and the Tiger.* Putnam, 1993.

King-Smith, Dick. *Three Terrible Trins.* Crown, 1994.

Kipling, Rudyard. "The Elephant's Child." In *Just So Stories.* Illustrated by Barry Moser. Morrow, 1996.

Lexau, Joan. *Crocodile and Hen: A Bakongo Folktale.* Rev. ed. Illustrated by Doug Cushman. HarperCollins, 2001.

London, Jonathan. *Master Elk and the Mountain Lion.* Illustrated by Wayne McLoughlin. Crown, 1995.

————. *Panther: Shadow of the Swamp.* Illustrated by Paul Morin. Candlewick, 2000.

Mayer, Mercer. *There's an Alligator under My Bed.* Dial, 1987.

Silverstein, Shel. *Lafcadio, the Lion Who Shot Back.* HarperCollins, 1963.

Souhami, Jessica. *No Dinner!* Marshall Cavendish, 1999.

Strasser, Todd. *Gator Prey.* Pocket, 1999.

Temple, Francis. *Tiger Soup.* Orchard, 1994.

TEN

Big and Bad

Monsters, Witches, Ghosts, and Other Creepy Characters

Lesson Plan at a Glance

OPENING POEM:	"Blood-Curdling Story" from *Falling Up* by Shel Silverstein
CHAPTER BOOK SELECTION:	*Coraline* by Neil Gaiman
PICTURE BOOK:	*Piggie Pie!* by Margie Palatini
POEM:	"I'm a Crotchety Witch" from *Monday's Troll* by Jack Prelutsky
PICTURE BOOK:	*The Lima Bean Monster* by Dan Yaccarino
ORAL TALE:	"Odon the Giant" from *Nursery Tales around the World* by Judy Sierra
PICTURE BOOK:	*A Big, Spooky House* by Donna Washington
POEM:	"Mary Had a Vampire Bat" from *Monster Goose* by Judy Sierra
READER'S THEATER:	"The Boy Who Wanted the Willies" from *Folktales on Stage: Sixteen Scripts for Reader's Theater from Folk and Fairy Tales of the World* by Aaron Shepard
PICTURE BOOK:	*Velcome* by Kevin O'Malley
DRAWING ACTIVITY:	Drawing Something Scary

Preparation and Presentation

Decorate the story area with ideas from the following book:

Sadler, Linda. *101 Spooktacular Party Ideas: Fun Halloween Recipes, Games, Decorations, and Craft Ideas for Ghosts and Ghouls of All Ages.* Creative Kids, 2000.

> This is one of the best of the many Halloween party planning books on the market. Use the decorating ideas, edible treats, games, and craft ideas for scary programs any time of the year.

OPENING POEM

Silverstein, Shel. "Blood-Curdling Story." In *Falling Up*. HarperCollins, 1996.

> This short poem starts the program on the right track with the narrator describing how scary a particular story is and begs for it to be told again. The poem is also found in
>
> > Stine, R. L. *Beware! R. L. Stine Picks His Favorite Scary Stories.* HarperCollins, 2002.

CHAPTER BOOK SELECTION

Gaiman, Neil. *Coraline*. HarperCollins, 2002.

> Set up this story by telling your audience that a young girl named Coraline discovers a passage to another house just like her own with some unsettling differences. Read the end of chapter 1 from the sentence "That night Coraline lay awake in her bed" to the end of the chapter. Start up again in chapter 3, when Coraline is home alone and she meets her "other mother." Begin this selection where she approaches the locked door in the drawing room—"The old black key felt colder than any of the others"—to the end of the chapter. Finish by stating that Coraline returns to her real house but discovers her real parents are missing.

PICTURE BOOK

Palatini, Margie. *Piggie Pie!* Illustrated by Howard Fine. Clarion, 1995.

> Now that your audience is creeped out, break the tension with this humorous story of Gritch the Witch, who desires Piggie Pie. She has most of the ingredients—an eye of a fly, two shakes of a rattlesnake's rattle, and three belly hairs of a possum. However, she's missing the most important parts of

her recipe—eight plump piggies. She heads over to Old MacDonald's Farm, "Just over the River and through the Woods," but is outsmarted by the clever pigs. The language is fun to read aloud. "Look, Shorty, I've been quack-quacked here, moo-mooed there, and cluck-clucked everywhere all over the farm." Gritch appears in the following fun sequels:

Palatini, Margie. *Broom Mates.* Illustrated by Howard Fine. Clarion, 2003.

————. *Zoom Broom.* Illustrated by Howard Fine. Clarion, 1998.

POEM

Prelutsky, Jack. "I'm a Crotchety Witch." In *Monday's Troll.* Greenwillow, 1996.

Follow the Palatini picture book about a witch in a funny situation with this poem about a witch in a funny situation. The crotchety, lonely witch celebrates her 30,303rd birthday. Other strong poems from this collection include "Ogrebrag," in which an ogre comments about his battle with a brave knight ("His horse was tasty, too"); "Mother Ogre's Lullaby" ("Close your red eye"); and the title tune, which is a takeoff on the traditional "Monday's Child" rhyme.

PICTURE BOOK

Yaccarino, Dan. *The Lima Bean Monster.* Illustrated by Adam McCauley. Walker, 2001.

Who loves lima beans? Not Sammy. He sneaks them off of his plate and buries them in a vacant lot. His friends start adding their least favorite items in the hole. When a bolt of lightning strikes the mound of dirt, a Lima Bean Monster is unleashed on the neighborhood.

ORAL TALE

Sierra, Judy. "Odon the Giant." In *Nursery Tales around the World.* Illustrated by Stefano Vitale. Clarion, 1996.

A little picoy bird, a mosquito, a crab, and a bedbug defeat a mean giant. This story from the Philippines is fun to act out as the giant. As you tell the story, mime the motions of the giant trying to swat the mosquito (but instead hitting his head), jumping up from being bitten by the bedbug, rubbing his eyes as the picoy bird flaps ashes on his face, and having the crab grab his lips when the giant plunges his face into the wash basin.

PICTURE BOOK

Washington, Donna. *A Big, Spooky House.* Illustrated by Jacqueline Rogers. Hyperion, 2000.

> A big, strong man is not afraid of anything, not even spending the night in "some-spooky-house-sitting-up-on-a-big-spooky-hill." Bigger and bigger cats appear and ask the big, strong man, "Are you gonna be here when John gets here?" Have the audience join in on the lines, "He was a BIG man! He was a STRONG man!" The story ends with the added line, "He was a GONE man!" This version of the traditional story "Wait Until Martin Comes" appears in a shorter version in the following collection:
>
> > Schwartz, Alvin. *Scary Stories to Tell in the Dark.* HarperCollins, 1981.

POEM

Sierra, Judy. "Mary Had a Vampire Bat." In *Monster Goose.* Harcourt, 2001.

> Have a construction-paper bat behind your back (a pattern can be found in Sadler's *101 Spooktacular Party Ideas,* listed earlier in this chapter). Pull it out when reading the line about Mary bringing her bat for show-and-tell. Other highlights from *Monster Goose* include the poems "There Was an Old Zombie" and "Twinkle, Twinkle, Little Slug."

READER'S THEATER

Shepard, Aaron. "The Boy Who Wanted the Willies." In *Folktales on Stage: Children's Plays for Reader's Theater.* Shepard Productions, 2003.

> This traditional Brothers Grimm story is similar to the Washington picture book; the main character shows no fear when confronted with scary characters in a spooky house. There are some fun differences. This protagonist has never been frightened in his life, and he wants to experience "the willies." He encounters a vampire, a werewolf, a line of skeletons, and a giant. Shepard generously allows commercial-free groups to copy and perform this script, which can also be found at www.aaronshep.com.

PICTURE BOOK

O'Malley, Kevin. *Velcome.* Walker, 1997.

> Instead of reading the entire book, I read the short "groaner-of-a-story" titled "Didja." A creepy, whispery voice calls out "Didja" before there is a

knock at the door and the punch line, "Didja order a pizza?" I wind up the story portion of the program by threatening the audience with the most frightening thing of all—a plate of mixed vegetables—as "horribly" portrayed in a two-page color spread by O'Malley.

DRAWING ACTIVITY

Drawing Something Scary

Challenge the audience to draw something scarier than the plate of mixed vegetables in O'Malley's picture book. Provide paper and art supplies. Set out drawing books, such as the following:

> Ames, Lee. *Draw Fifty Beasties and Yugglies and Turnover Uglies and Things That Go Bump in the Night.* Doubleday, 1988.
>
> ———. *Draw Fifty Monsters, Creeps, Superheroes, Demons, Dragons, Nerds, Dirts, Ghouls, Giants, Vampires, Zombies, and Other Curiosa.* Doubleday, 1983.
>
> Emberley, Ed. *Ed Emberley's Drawing Book of Weirdos.* Little, Brown, 2002.
>
> ———. *Ed Emberley's Halloween Drawing Book.* Little, Brown, 1995.

You may prefer to have the kids make some of the crafts found in the Sadler *101 Spooktacular Party Ideas* book or one of the following resource books:

> Biddle, Steve. *Origami Monsters.* Barron's, 2001.
>
> Ross, Kathy. *Make Yourself a Monster! A Book of Creepy Crafts.* Millbrook, 1999.

Mix and Match Picture Books

Ashman, Linda. *The Essential Worldwide Monster Guide.* Illustrated by David Small. Simon and Schuster, 2003.

These humorous poems feature many lesser-known mythological creatures from various cultures, such as the Alicanto from South America, the Ki-Lin from China, and the Abatwa from Africa.

Compton, Kenn, and Joanne Compton. *Jack the Giant Chaser.* Holiday House, 1993.

Jack kills seven catfish with one rock. The townsfolk are impressed and ask Jack to rid the land of the local giant.

Johnston, Tony. *Alice Nizzy Nazzy: The Witch of Santa Fe*. Illustrated by Tomie DePaola. Putnam, 1995.

This Southwest U.S. version of the Baba Yaga legend features a somewhat-scary, yellow-skinned, chili-haired witch who throws little Manuela into a pot.

McCaughrean, Geraldine. *Grandma Chickenlegs*. Illustrated by Moira Kemp. Carolrhoda, 1999.

This is one of the better Baba Yaga picture books in print. Tatia's mean stepmother sends her to fetch a needle from Grandma Chickenlegs. There are great pictures of the green-skinned, green-fingernailed witch, complete with bat glasses and spider earrings (and, in one memorable shot, her hair done up in rollers). Once Tatia escapes, Grandma Chickenlegs climbs back in her house made of chicken legs and goes "to another country, another story, another secret corner of the tall-tale world."

Reeves, Howard. *There Was an Old Witch*. Illustrated by David Catrow. Hyperion, 1998.

This is a witchy version of "I Know an Old Lady Who Swallowed a Fly." "There was an old witch who wanted a bat / I know why she wanted the bat / But I won't tell you that." She wants the bat to adorn her Halloween hat. As you read the concluding line, set a witch hat, complete with a cutout bat decoration, on your head.

San Souci, Robert D. *Cinderella Skeleton*. Illustrated by David Catrow. Harcourt, 2000.

Cinderella's stepsisters mistreat her. They make her work hard hanging up cobwebs, arranging dead flowers, and littering the floor with dust and leaves. When she hurries from the ball, she leaves behind her whole skeletal foot.

Sierra, Judy. *The Dancing Pig*. Illustrated by Jesse Sweetwater. Harcourt, 1999.

A pig, a mouse, and some frogs help a mother rescue her twin daughters from the terrible ogress Rangsasa. This Indonesian folktale is rich in language and onomatopoeic noises.

Sierra, Judy. *Tasty Baby Belly Buttons*. Illustrated by Meilo So. Knopf, 1999.

Horrible monsters known as "oni" terrorize Japan, "kidnapping children in order to find their favorite treat—belly buttons." A little warrior girl and her animal companions save the day. The audience can help recite the onis' cry, "Belly buttons / Belly buttons / Tasty belly buttons."

Wood, Audrey. *Heckedy Peg.* Illustrated by Don Wood. Harcourt, 1987.

A witch changes seven children into different types of food. In order to save them, their mother is forced to correctly guess which food item is which child. This story makes for a good visual presentation, such as a felt-board or prop story, with pieces made up of the seven children being exchanged for the pieces of food and the unique objects the mother brings to identify the children.

Mix and Match Chapter Book Selections

Dahl, Roald. *The Witches.* Farra, Straus and Giroux, 1983.

A boy and his grandmother dare to take on the Grand High Witch of the World and her followers. Read the chapters titled "How to Recognize a Witch" and "Frizzled Like a Fritter." This is a delightfully creepy, modern-day classic.

Naylor, Phyllis Reynolds. *Witch's Sister.* Atheneum, 1975.

Lynn and Mouse suspect that another girl, Judith, and old Mrs. Tuggle are witches. Read a portion of chapter 2, beginning with "The Tuggle house sat at the very top of the hill" to the end of the chapter. Lynn and Mouse witness the other two stabbing pins in a doll. Later that night, Mouse experiences a stomachache.

Shan, Darren. *Cirque du Freak: The Saga of Darren Shan, Book 1.* Little, Brown, 2001.

This book is filled with cliff-hangers perfect for reading aloud. Darren and Steve attend a mysterious freak show. Read chapter 8, which leads up to the start of the dangerous show. This chapter ends with the line, "That was when the screaming began." If time allows, read chapter 15. Steve confronts an actual vampire.

Mix and Match Short Story Selections

Stine, R. L. *Beware! R. L. Stine Picks His Favorite Scary Stories.* HarperCollins, 2002.

Take your pick of several scary stories by such notable authors as Bram Stoker, Patricia McKissack, William Sleator, Leon Garfield, Alvin Schwartz, and more. My favorite is Ray Bradbury's "The Black Ferris."

Mix and Match Oral Tales

Hamilton, Virginia. "Baba Yaga, the Terrible." In *The Dark Way: Stories from the Spirit World*. Harcourt, 1990.

Yet another fine retelling of the evil Russian witch story.

MacDonald, Margaret Read. "The Tinker and the Ghost." In *When the Lights Go Out: Twenty Scary Tales to Tell*. Wilson, 1988.

A ghost's legs fall down the chimney, then its trunk, its arms, and finally its head. Have fun with the ghost's yell, "OOOOHHH MEEeee . . . OOOOHHH MEEeee . . . LOOK OUT BELOWWW . . . I'M FALLINGGG . . ."

San Souci, Robert D. "Witch Woman." In *Even More Short and Shivery: Thirty Spine-Tingling Stories*. Delacorte, 1997.

An exhausted traveler spends the night in an old woman's cabin. The woman turns out to be a witch who can shed her human skin and turn into a panther. The traveler escapes by pouring pepper and salt into her "witch woman skin."

Mix and Match Poetry

Bolsta, Phil. "The Monsters in My Closet." In *Kids Pick the Funniest Poems*. Edited by Bruce Lansky. Illustrated by Stephen Carpenter. Meadowbrook, 1991.

cummings, e. e. "Hist Whist." In *The Twentieth Century Children's Poetry Treasury*. Edited by Jack Prelutsky. Illustrated by Meilo So. Knopf, 1999.

Dugan, Michael. "Tables Turned." In *A Bad Case of the Giggles*. Edited by Bruce Lansky. Illustrated by Stephen Carpenter. Meadowbrook, 1994.

Duggan, Paul. "Two Skeletons on the Telephone" and "A Vampire Bit a Ghostly Neck." In *Two Skeletons on the Telephone and Other Poems from Tough City*. Illustrated by Daniel Sylvestre. Millbrook, 1999.

Fishback, Margaret. "Hallowe'en Indignation Meeting." In *Tomie DePaola's Book of Poems*. Edited and illustrated by Tomie DePaola. Putnam, 1988.

Florian, Douglas. "Beware the Beast," "Hello, My Name Is Dracula," and "Ogres Are Ugly." In *Laugh-eteria*. Harcourt, 1999.

Hall, Willis. "Believing." In *Kids Pick the Funniest Poems*. Edited by Bruce Lansky. Illustrated by Stephen Carpenter. Meadowbrook, 1991.

Katz, Bobbi. "The Witch's Invitation." In *A Rumpus of Rhymes: A Book of Noisy Poems*. Illustrated by Susan Estelle Kwas. Dutton, 2001.

Kennedy, X. J. "Whose Boo Is Whose?" and "Wicked Witch Admires Herself." In *Exploding Gravy: Poems to Make You Laugh*. Illustrated by Joy Allen. Little, Brown, 2002.

Prelutsky, Jack. "I Am a Ghost Who Lost His Boo." In *Something Big Has Been Here*. Illustrated by James Stevenson. Greenwillow, 1990.

Silverstein, Shel. "Haunted" and "Setting Around." In *Falling Up*. HarperCollins, 1996.

Spinelli, Eileen. "I Don't Believe in Bigfoot." In *The Twentieth Century Children's Poetry Treasury*. Edited by Jack Prelutsky. Illustrated by Meilo So. Knopf, 1999.

Viorst, Judith. ". . . And While Poor Hansel Was Locked in the Witch's Cage, Awaiting His Doom, Clever Gretel Came to Her Brother's Rescue" and "That Old Haunted House." In *Sad Underwear and Other Complications*. Illustrated by Richard Hull. Atheneum, 1995.

Tweaking the Program Theme . . .

. . . For Preschoolers

Drop the Gaiman chapter book selection and the Shepard reader's theater presentation, and substitute the following picture books:

Kasza, Keiko. *Grandpa Toad's Secret*. Putnam, 1995.

> Grandpa Toad shares his secrets for facing dangerous enemies, such as snakes, snapping turtles, and monsters.

Melmed, Laura Krauss. *Fright Night Flight*. Illustrated by Henry Cole. HarperCollins, 2002.

> Witch makes room on her super jet-fueled broom for a vampire, a werewolf, a ghost, a monster, a skeleton, and a mummy.

. . . For Fifth and Sixth Graders

Drop the Yaccarino picture book, and substitute the following chapter book selection:

Hahn, Mary Downing. *Wait till Helen Comes.* Clarion, 1986.

> This is still the first title I recommend to that upper-elementary student who asks for "a REAL scary book." Michael and Molly fear their new stepsister, Heather, and her ghostly companion, Helen. Read chapter 9. Heather gets her siblings in trouble and warns them, "Just wait till Helen comes. You'll be sorry…"

And Yet Even More Books about Monsters, Witches, Ghosts, and Other Creepy Characters for You to Consider

Cuyler, Margery. *Skeleton Hiccups.* Illustrated by S. D. Schindler. Margaret K. McElderry, 2002.

Galdone, Paul. *The Monster and the Tailor.* Clarion, 1982.

Johnson, Paul Brett. *A Perfect Pork Stew.* Orchard, 1998.

Mayer, Mercer. *Liza Lou and the Yeller Belly Swamp.* Parents' Magazine, 1976.

Numeroff, Laura Joffe. *Laura Numeroff's Ten-Step Guide to Living with Your Monster.* Illustrated by Nate Evans. HarperCollins, 2002.

Reiner, Carl. *Tell Me a Scary Story—But Not Too Scary!* Illustrated by James Bennett. Little, Brown, 2003.

Rockwell, Anne. *The One-Eyed Giant and Other Monsters from the Greek Myths.* Greenwillow, 1996.

Schwartz, Alvin. *Ghosts! Ghostly Tales from Folklore.* Illustrated by Victoria Chess. HarperCollins, 1991.

———. *In a Dark, Dark Room and Other Scary Stories.* Illustrated by Dirk Zimmer. HarperCollins, 1984.

Viorst, Judith. *My Mama Says There Aren't Any Zombies, Ghosts, Vampires, Creatures, Demons, Monsters, Fiends, Goblins, or Things.* Illustrated by Kay Chorao. Atheneum, 1973.

Wahl, Jan. *Tailypo!* Illustrated by Wil Clay. Henry Holt, 1991.

Williams, Linda. *The Little Old Lady Who Was Not Afraid of Anything.* Illustrated by Megan Lloyd. Crowell, 1986.

Yep, Laurence. *The Man Who Tricked a Ghost.* Illustrated by Isadore Seltzer. Bridgewater, 1993.

ELEVEN

A Good Frog Story

Lesson Plan at a Glance

PICTURE BOOK:	*The Big Wide-Mouthed Frog* by Ana Martin Larranaga
SHORT STORY SELECTION:	"The Celebrated Jumping Frog of Calavaras County" by Mark Twain
CHAPTER BOOK SELECTION:	*Leap, Frog* by Jane Cutler
POEM:	"The Great Frog Race" from *The Great Frog Race and Other Poems* by Kristine O'Connell George
PICTURE BOOK:	*Fribbity Ribbit!* by Suzanne C. Johnson
POEM:	"Polliwogs" from *The Great Frog Race and Other Poems* by Kristine O'Connell George
SHORT STORY SELECTION:	"A Boy and His Frog" from *Ribbiting Tales* by David Lubar
PICTURE BOOK:	*Once There Was a Bull . . . Frog* by Rick Walton
ORAL TALE:	"How Br'er Rabbit Outsmarted the Frogs," retold by Jackie Torrence from *African-American Folktales for Young Readers* by Richard Young and Judy Dockrey Young
READER'S THEATER:	Selections from *Frantic Frogs and Other Frankly Fractured Folktales for Readers Theater* by Anthony D. Fredericks

Preparation and Presentation

Decorate the story program area with pictures of frogs on lily pads modeled after those found in David Wiesner's award-winning picture book *Tuesday* (Clarion, 1991). Start the program by asking the audience to make a variety of frog noises, from "Ribit" to "Croak."

PICTURE BOOK

Martin Larranaga, Ana. *The Big Wide-Mouthed Frog.* Candlewick, 1999.

> This very popular traditional story is now set in Australia. A big wide-mouthed frog encounters a kangaroo, a koala, a possum, an emu, and a crocodile. He asks each creature, "Who are you and what do you eat?" He manages to get in a few insults, too, calling the kangaroo "Big Thumping Feet" and the koala "Mr. Big Nose." Of course, in the end, the crocodile, aka "Knobby Brown Log," replies that he eats big wide-mouthed frogs. Read the frog's lines very loud until he gives his tight-lipped response that he is actually "a small narrow-mouthed frog." I have a balloon-prop version of this story in my book *Family Storytime* (ALA, 1999).

SHORT STORY SELECTION

Twain, Mark. "The Celebrated Jumping Frog of Calavaras County." (Any edition.)

> Smiley is the bragging owner of the frog Dan'l Webster. One day, a stranger arrives in camp and listens to Smiley boast of Dan'l Webster's jumping prowess. They decide to bet $40 to see whose frog can outjump the other. When Smiley goes off to fetch his competitor a frog, the stranger fills Dan'l Webster with quail shot, making the frog "as solid as an anvil." This classic story can be found not only in several anthologies, but also in full text online on various sites. Type the title in any search engine.

CHAPTER BOOK SELECTION

Cutler, Jane. *Leap, Frog.* Farrar, Straus and Giroux, 2002.

> A group of kids host a frog-jumping contest after hearing a teacher read Twain's "The Celebrated Jumping Frog of Calavaras County." Read the chapter titled after the book and begin with the sentence, "'And now,' said Janice into the microphone . . ." Read through the action where Edward and Charley's frog jumps farther than any other frog, but it jumps the wrong

direction. Finish the selection on the line, "'But it jumped the farthest,' persisted Elaine."

POEM

George, Kristine O'Connell. "The Great Frog Race." In *The Great Frog Race and Other Poems*. Illustrated by Kate Kiesler. Clarion, 1997.

This poem is a nice companion piece to the Twain short story since it involves contesting frogs. Several people set down seventeen frogs and yell, "Ready . . . Set . . . Go!" Unfortunately for the humans, the frogs scatter in all directions, bringing the race to a quick end.

PICTURE BOOK

Johnson, Suzanne C. *Fribbity Ribbit!* Illustrated by Debbie Tilley. Knopf, 2001.

Like "The Great Frog Race" poem, this story line involves a frog in a race—a race to avoid getting caught by several humans. The frog starts in the backyard and then hops into Dad's garage, Grandpa's kitchen, Dog's bowl, Granny's office, Sister's bath, Baby's train, Brother's room, Mama's studio, and winds up once again in the backyard. This is a fun, tongue-twisting text.

POEM

George, Kristine O'Connell. "Polliwogs." In *The Great Frog Race and Other Poems*. Illustrated by Kate Kiesler. Clarion, 1997.

Read this short poem that describes the little polliwogs as "chubby commas" and "frogs-in-waiting." This poem is a good lead-in to the next short story since it shows how frogs start out so little.

SHORT STORY SELECTION

Lubar, David. "A Boy and His Frog." In *Ribbiting Tales*. Edited by Nancy Springer. Philomel, 2000.

A boy's pet frog, Jumpy, becomes so huge that he swallows one of Mrs. Munsinger's Chihuahuas. The boy hauls Jumpy to Bear Creek Swamp, where, soon afterward, all of the wildlife disappears. The boy creates Buzzella, a fly the size of a vulture, and brings it, along with several similar flies, to the swamp. This funny and slightly twisted story ends with the boy's concern about his new ant farm.

PICTURE BOOK

Walton, Rick. *Once There Was a Bull . . . Frog*. Illustrated by Greg Hally.
  Gibbs-Smith, 1995.

  A bullfrog goes off in search of his missing hop. This series of wordplay and
  visual fun has the audience guessing the second half of compound words.
  For example, when the frog lands "hard in a patch of grass," we turn the
  page and learn that he lands among "grasshoppers" that resemble the patch
  of grass. The story ends with the frog eating a horse . . . fly.

ORAL TALE

Torrence, Jackie. "How Br'er Rabbit Outsmarted the Frogs." In *African-
  American Folktales for Young Readers*. Edited by Richard Young and Judy
  Dockrey Young. August House, 1993.

  This very popular traditional story relates how Br'er Rabbit helped Br'er
  Coon grab a bunch of frogs. Br'er Rabbit asks the frogs to help dig a hole to
  bury Br'er Coon, who is lying on the ground, apparently dead. The frogs dig
  and dig until the hole is too deep for them to jump out. Then, and only then,
  does Br'er Coon spring up and start throwing frogs "into that tow sack."
  Versions of the same story can be found in the following collections:

> Holt, David, and Bill Mooney. "Is It Deep Enough?" In *Ready-to-
> Tell Tales*. August House, 1994.

> Lester, Julius. "Brer Rabbit, Brer Coon, and the Frogs." In *More
> Tales of Uncle Remus*. Dial, 1988.

READER'S THEATER

Fredericks, Anthony D. *Frantic Frogs and Other Frankly Fractured Folktales for
  Readers Theater*. Libraries Unlimited, 1993.

  Distribute copies of these very short, ready-to-reproduce scripts to your
  audience. If you have enough kids who can read, they can get into small
  groups and look over their lines. Once everyone has had a few minutes, they
  can take turns reading the plays to the whole audience or perhaps at a later
  library or school program that includes parents and younger children.
  Fredericks's book contains the following frog-themed stories:

> "Don't Kiss Us, We're Just a Bunch of Frogs" (five roles for readers);

> "The Frog Princess (and What About All Those Frog Princes?)"
>   (seven roles);

"Mr. Toad: Just Another One of Those Crazy Amphibians" (five roles);

"Picture This: It's a Photo Opportunity" (three roles);

"The Semi-Confused Prince Who Lived in a Very Large Castle by a Big Cruddy Swamp Filled with Funny Green Amphibians" (seven roles); and

"So, Who Is This Kermit Guy, Anyway?" (four roles).

Mix and Match Picture Books

Hightower, Susan. *Twelve Snails to One Lizard.* Illustrated by Matt Novak. Simon and Schuster, 1997.

Beaver is building his dam and needs Frog's help with measurements. After Beaver tries to line up inch-long snails, foot-long lizards, and one yard-long snake, he blows his top when Frog produces a regular yardstick.

Wood, Audrey. *Jubal's Wish.* Illustrated by Don Wood. Scholastic, 2000.

Jubal Bullfrog unselfishly wishes for good things to happen to Gerdy Toad and Captain Dalbert Lizard. The wishes do not happen as planned but finally succeed in a roundabout manner.

Mix and Match Chapter Book Selection

Napoli, Donna Jo. *The Prince of the Pond.* Dutton, 1992.

A wicked witch turns a prince into a frog. Read the opening chapter, "The Hag." A female frog comes across the stunned, newly transformed prince-frog. While she tries to help the prince, the witch returns to the scene threatening to eat the frog.

Mix and Match Short Stories

Harris, Robert J. "Old Croaker Jumps over the Moon." In *Ribbiting Tales.* Edited by Nancy Springer. Philomel, 2000.

This original tall tale concerns a frog that learns to leap up to the Moon, attach itself to the Moon's eye with its tongue, and spiral back down to Earth—all for the attention of the attractive Miss Pollywog Pearl.

Mix and Match Oral Tales

Klein, Susan. "Little Frog and Centipede." In *More Ready-to-Tell Tales from around the World*. Edited by David Holt and Bill Mooney. August House, 2000.

Little Frog impatiently interrupts Centipede's explanation of how she gets her skin so shiny. She finally leaves in a huff before Little Frog gets all of the correct information. He asks his mother to boil some oil and then jumps in. This is why frogs have such ugly skin to this day.

Lester, Julius. "Brer Fox Gets Tricked by the Frogs" and "Brer Bear Gets Tricked by Brer Frog." In *Further Tales of Uncle Remus: The Misadventures of Brer Rabbit, Brer Fox, Brer Wolf, the Doodlebug, and Other Creatures*. Dial, 1990.

These very short tales are connected as first Brer Bullfrog gets Brer Fox wet and then Brer Frog saves his own skin from an angry Brer Bear.

Lester, Julius. "Brer Rabbit and Brer Bullfrog." In *More Tales of Uncle Remus: Further Adventures of Brer Rabbit, His Friends, Enemies, and Others*. Dial, 1988.

Brer Frog tricks Brer Rabbit into falling into water where he "sneezed and snozed and snozed and sneezed" to the frog's amusement. Brer Rabbit plots revenge. This story explains why frogs no longer have tails.

Spelman. Jon. "The Snake and the Frog." In *More Ready-to-Tell Tales from around the World*. Edited by David Holt and Bill Mooney. August House, 2000.

Two men bet on whether a snake will eat an enormous frog or if the frog will eat the snake. The two creatures start eating each other until—with each giving one final bite—they both vanish.

Tweaking the Program Theme . . .

. . . *For Preschoolers*

Drop the Cutler chapter book selection, the Fredericks reader's theater activity, and the Twain short story, and substitute the following picture books:

Burris, Priscilla. *Five Green and Speckled Frogs*. Cartwheel, 2003.

This colorful picture book is based on a popular traditional counting song. "Five green and speckled frogs / sitting on a speckled log / eating some most delicious bugs . . ." Use it in conjunction with Raffi's musical version from one of his recordings:

The Raffi Singable Songs Collection. Rounder, 1988.

Singable Songs for the Very Young. Rounder, 1976.

Wilson, Karma. *A Frog in the Bog.* Illustrated by Joan Rankin. Margaret K. McElderry, 2003.

A frog sitting on a log swallows a litany of critters, starting with ONE tick, TWO fleas, THREE flies, FOUR slugs, and winding up with FIVE snails before realizing the log is actually an alligator.

Yolen, Jane. *Hoptoad.* Illustrated by Karen Lee Schmidt. Harcourt, 2003.

A toad crosses a desert road at the same time as a lizard and tortoise. A pickup truck threatens to squash the slow-moving toad and create a "toad-al disaster."

. . . For Fifth and Sixth Graders

Drop the Johnson picture book, and substitute the following oral tale:

Bruchac, Joseph. "The Woman Who Married a Frog." In *Native American Animal Stories.* Fulcrum, 1992.

This strange but compelling story from the Inuit culture of the Pacific Northwest focuses on the daughter of the town chief who insults a frog for being ugly. A handsome man arrives shortly afterward and announces he will marry her. He is the insulted frog in disguise. The frog-man leads her underwater to the Frog People. The young woman's parents appeal to the frogs to return their daughter but to no avail. The humans finally get her back through the use of force. To this day, the daughter's people treat frogs with respect.

And Yet Even More Froggy Books for You to Consider

Ada, Alma Flor. *Friend Frog.* Illustrated by Lori Lohstoeter. Harcourt, 2000.

Anderson, Peggy Perry. *Out to Lunch.* Houghton Mifflin, 1998.

Arnold, Tedd. *Green Wilma.* Dial, 1993.

Chang, Heidi. *Elaine and the Flying Frog*. Random House, 1988.

Conford, Ellen. *The Frog Princess of Pelham*. Little, Brown, 1997.

Duke, Kate. *Seven Froggies Went to School*. Dutton, 1985.

Grobler, Piet. *Hey, Frog!* Front Street, 2002.

Joyce, William. *Bently & Egg*. HarperCollins, 1992.

Lionni, Leo. *An Extraordinary Egg*. Knopf, 1994.

———. *It's Mine!* Knopf, 1986.

Priceman, Marjorie. *Friend or Frog?* Houghton Mifflin, 1989.

Shannon, George. *April Showers*. Illustrated by Jose Aruego and Ariane Dewey. Greenwillow, 1995.

———. *Frog Legs: A Picture Book of Action Verse*. Illustrated by Amit Trynan. Greenwillow, 2000.

Steig, William. *Gorky Rises*. Farrar, Straus and Giroux, 1980.

Winer, Yvonne. *Frogs Sing Songs*. Illustrated by Tony Oliver. Charlesbridge, 2003.

Yolen, Jane. *King Long Shanks*. Illustrated by Victoria Chess. Harcourt, 1998.

TWELVE

Rats!

Lesson Plan at a Glance

PICTURE BOOK:	*That Pesky Rat* by Lauren Child
PICTURE BOOK:	*Three by the Sea* by Edward Marshall
CHAPTER BOOK SELECTION:	*The Tale of Despereaux* by Kate DiCamillo
PICTURE BOOK:	*Slim and Jim* by Richard Egielski
PICTURE BOOK/ORAL TALE:	*Cat and Rat: The Legend of the Chinese Zodiac* by Ed Young
CHAPTER BOOK SELECTION:	*Rats on the Roof and Other Stories* by James Marshall
POEM:	"Rat for Lunch!" from *A Pizza the Size of the Sun* by Jack Prelutsky
ACTIVITY:	Visit from a Live Rat

Preparation and Presentation

Start the program by displaying color photos of rats from the following nonfiction books:

Conniff, Richard. *Rats! The Good, the Bad and the Ugly.* Crown, 2002.

Display the endpaper color photos of a multitude of real rats crawling over each other.

Simon, Seymour. *Animals Nobody Loves.* North-South, 2001.

> This will get reactions from the audience, as they enter the story area, rang-
> ing from "Ugh" to "Cool." It will also serve as a nice contrast to the ending
> activity of bringing a live pet rat to the program.

PICTURE BOOK

Child, Lauren. *That Pesky Rat.* Candlewick, 2002.

> A street rat will "do almost anything to be somebody's pet." With the coop-
> eration of the pet store owner, he even posts a sign in the window and adds
> in small print, "not a very good picture of me." Mr. Fortesque takes the rat
> home thinking that it's a cat. The rat does not correct him. Have fun read-
> ing the tricky text that is sometimes intertwined with the illustrations.

PICTURE BOOK

Marshall, Edward. *Three by the Sea.* Illustrated by James Marshall. Dial, 1981.

> Read the chapter "Sam's Story." A rat goes to a pet shop to buy a cat. "'Are
> you sure you want a cat?' asked the owner." As the rat and cat get to know
> each other, the rat innocently asks, "What is your favorite dish?" The end-
> ing might come as a surprise to the audience.

CHAPTER BOOK SELECTION

DiCamillo, Kate. *The Tale of Despereaux.* Candlewick, 2003.

> This Newbery Award winner is already an instant classic with the school-
> age crowd. Despereaux is a little mouse that is sentenced to a horrible death
> of being eaten by rats in the dungeon. The selected chapters are very short,
> but the language flows off each page and is fun to read aloud. Start with
> chapter 8, "To the Rats." The narrator asks the reader to look up the word
> *perfidy* in the dictionary. Interrupt the story long enough to allow the audi-
> ence members to do so (have a handy dictionary in the story area). Continue
> to read chapter 10, "Good Reasons," which ends with Despereaux fainting.
> Finally, read chapter 14, "Darkness." In the dungeon, Despereaux hears
> what he believes is the voice of a rat, and "for the second time that day, the
> mouse fainted."

PICTURE BOOK

Egielski, Richard. *Slim and Jim.* HarperCollins, 2002.

> As we learned from the DiCamillo story, rats are sometimes menacing to
> mice in children's stories. This picture book, however, portrays Slim the rat

and Jim the mouse as good buddies. Yo-yo buddies, in fact. They deal with Buster, an evil one-eyed cat. The story has a Charles Dickens–adventure feel to it. The exciting climax involves all three characters high on a rooftop. There's also a bonus for Beatles fans: Slim has a yo-yo that plays "Ob-La-Di, Ob-La-Da."

PICTURE BOOK/ORAL TALE

Young, Ed. *Cat and Rat: The Legend of the Chinese Zodiac.* Holt, 1995.

Not only does this legend explain how the Chinese zodiac came to be, but also why cats and rats are enemies. Once upon a time, they were best friends. But selfish Rat shoved Cat during the great animal race. Rat finished first, and poor Cat did not even place in the top twelve places. This story will be easier to memorize if the storyteller has a print copy of the Chinese zodiac nearby to refer to the various animals and the places they finished in the race.

CHAPTER BOOK SELECTION

Marshall, James. *Rats on the Roof and Other Stories.* Dial, 1991.

Not all cats are good at catching rats. Otis and Sophie Dog have a problem. They have rats on their roof that dance and play music all night long. Desperate, they advertise for a cat. The cat that shows up proves to be a bigger problem than the rats. When the cat finally learns that the Dogs have rats, he screams out, "They've got RATS in here! Somebody do something. Call 911!" In the morning, the Dogs find a note from the rats complaining of the noise.

POEM

Prelutsky, Jack. "Rat for Lunch!" In *A Pizza the Size of the Sun.* Illustrated by James Stevenson. Greenwillow, 1996.

There's nothing like a rat to eat for lunch. It's better than "scrambled slug in salty slime," "bits of baked baboon," and similar delicacies. This is one of those poems that gets a reaction from the kids on each and every line. The poem will be enhanced if you pretend to nibble on a rubber or puppet rat (but not with your next guest, the live rat).

ACTIVITY

Visit from a Live Rat

Make arrangements with a local pet shop owner or someone who owns a pet rat to bring in a rat for the kids to see and pet. Allow for a question-and-answer session so that the audience will learn the benefits of rats and how to care for them as a pet. Make sure to check with your library or school policy about live animals. Advertise the visit ahead of time in case there are allergies or other concerns.

Mix and Match Picture Books

Bang-Campbell, Monika. *Little Rat Sets Sail.* Illustrated by Molly Bang. Harcourt, 2002.

Little Rat is afraid of sailing lessons. She's afraid of being a dork and a scaredy-cat. As she slowly becomes "brave Little Rat," she and the audience learn several sailing terms, such as *prams, capsize, centerboard, tiller, mainsail, job,* and more.

Crimi, Carolyn. *Don't Need Friends.* Illustrated by Lynn Munsinger. Doubleday, 1999.

Rat and Dog make a point of yelling at each other to keep out of their respective ends of the junkyard. When Dog is sick, Rat slowly shows some compassion. After repeatedly stating that he doesn't need any friends, Rat finally says, "Don't need many friends . . . Just need one."

Fraser, Mary Ann. *I.Q. Goes to School.* Walker, 2002.

I.Q. the rat would rather be a student than the class pet. While waiting his turn to be the student of the week, he learns the alphabet along with the human kids. He also makes Halloween decorations, finger-paints a rainbow, acts in the school play, counts to ten, and more. If you use this picture book with a visit from a pet rat, you can ask the audience if they think the pet rat is as smart as I.Q.

Lester, Helen. *Hooway for Wodney Wat.* Illustrated by Lynn Munsinger. Houghton Mifflin, 1999.

Poor Wodney Wat's real name is Rodney Rat. He's unable to pronounce his Rs. The other rodents tease him. A new student named Camilla Capybara turns out to be a bully. When Wodney is selected as the leader of the game "Simon Says," Camilla misunderstands his directions and, much to the relief of Wodney and his classmates, heads out of their lives.

Meddaugh, Susan. *Cinderella's Rat.* Houghton Mifflin, 1997.

A rat is changed into Cinderella's coachman. A wizard turns the rat's sister into a human girl who says "Woof." When the clock strikes midnight, the coachman turns back into a rat. His sister, however, remains human and still barks. This is a clever fractured-fairy-tale adaptation of the Cinderella story.

Stevenson, James. *The Most Amazing Dinosaur.* Greenwillow, 2000.

Wilfred the rat sneaks into a museum to get out of the cold. Inside, he finds a host of small animals and birds living there in secret. They are thrown out when they wreck a display of dinosaur bones. When the critters attempt to correct their mistake, they create a very interesting interpretation of what dinosaurs looked and acted like in prehistoric times.

Mix and Match Chapter Book Selections

Avi. *The Christmas Rat.* Atheneum, 2000.

Eric is deputized to help a professional exterminator rid the apartment complex of a rat. It doesn't take long for Eric to wonder who is creepier: the rat or the exterminator. Read a portion of chapter 6. Start with the sentence, "Gabriel here!" and read until the end of the chapter.

Cutler, Jane. *Rats!* Farrar, Straus and Giroux, 1996.

The Frasier boys conduct experiments to learn if they are allergic to pet rats. Read the first part of the chapter titled "Rats!" until the sentence, "'Terrific!' said Rudy, clearing his scratchy throat a couple of times."

Jacques, Brian. *Redwall.* Philomel, 1987.

There are an amazing number of choices to read about evil rats in the various Redwall books. Why not start with the first rat Redwall fans met— Cluny the Scourge. Read the very short chapter 2, where we first meet Cluny, the most savage rat ever. Follow up by reading the last section of chapter 17. Matthias tries to rescue the Vole family with the help of the hilarious Basil Stag Hare. Begin with the sentence, "Would it be possible for you to create some kind of diversion while I'm getting the tapestry?" and read until the end of the chapter, where our heroes walk smack right into some sentry rats.

Pratchett, Terry. *The Amazing Maurice and His Educated Rodents.* HarperCollins, 2001.

Maurice, a talking cat, operates a Pied Piper scam. His rats invade a town, and his boy lures them away—for a fee. Read the opening chapter. The rats stop a highwayman from robbing them. This funny passage has the highwayman making sure his victims aren't wizards, witches, trolls, werewolves, or vampires.

Pullman, Philip. *I Was a Rat!* Knopf, 2000.

Ask your audience to imagine what might happen to one of the rats that was turned into Cinderella's pageboys. See what happens when one of the pageboys wanders off and doesn't change back to a rat. Read chapter 1. The rat that was turned into a boy turns up at a cobbler's house. The boy-rat tries to eat with a spoon and informs his hosts that he's only three weeks old. This is a good companion piece to Meddaugh's picture book *Cinderella's Rat*.

Mix and Match Oral Tale

Hamilton, Virginia. "The Cat and the Rat." In *A Ring of Tricksters: Animal Tales from America, the West Indies, and Africa*. Illustrated by Barry Moser. Scholastic, 1997.

Cat and Rat find a piece of cheese and ask Bruh Fox to divide it equally. Bruh Fox has other plans and insists on taking a little piece "for the judge." When Cat and Rat complain, Bruh Fox yips, barks, and lunges at the two. The moral of the story begins with "Finders, keepers; losers, weepers" and ends with "there's always less than honor among thieves."

Mix and Match Poetry

Duggan, Paul. "If You're Strolling in a Sewer," "Murphy the Rat," and "The Rat Catcher." In *Two Skeletons on the Telephone and Other Poems from Tough City*. Illustrated by Daniel Sylvestre. Millbrook, 1999.

McNaughton, Colin. "I Thought I'd Take My Rat to School." In *For Laughing Out Loud*. Edited by Jack Prelutsky. Illustrated by Marjorie Priceman. Knopf, 1991.

Prelutsky, Jack. "I Do Not Like the Rat!" In *The New Kid on the Block*. Illustrated by James Stevenson. Greenwillow, 1984.

———. "I Met a Rat of Culture." In *Something Big Has Been Here*. Illustrated by James Stevenson. Greenwillow, 1990.

Schertle, Alice. "A Traveler's Tale." In *Advice for a Frog*. Illustrated by Norman Green. Lothrop, Lee and Shepard, 1995.

Silverstein, Shel. "Drats." In *Where the Sidewalk Ends*. HarperCollins, 1974.

Tweaking the Program Theme . . .

. . . For Preschoolers

Drop DiCamillo's chapter book selection, and substitute the following picture book:

McPhail, David. *Big Brown Bear's Up and Down Day*. Harcourt, 2003.

> Rat keeps trying to get one of Big Brown Bear's slippers for a bed. He goes so far as to offer Bear a surprise vacation: "Any sort of trip you want." The two slowly become friends. Big Brown Bear eventually discovers one worn slipper that's just right for Rat's bed.

. . . For Fifth and Sixth Graders

Drop the two Marshall books, and substitute the following short story:

Yep, Laurence. "The Great Rat Hunt." In *When I Was Your Age: Original Stories about Growing Up*. Edited by Amy Ehrlich. Candlewick, 1996.

> A young boy tries to help his father kill a rat that has invaded their home. Armed with a rifle, the two flee when the rat charges them. During the hunt, the young narrator learns a few things about his father, who moved from China. Begin about two-thirds into the story with the sentence, "Now let's kill that rat," and read until the end.

And Yet Even More Books about Rats for You to Consider

Allen, Jeffrey. *Nosey Mrs. Rat*. Illustrated by James Marshall. Viking, 1985.

Bellows, Cathy. *Four Fat Rats*. Macmillan, 1987.

Bryan, Ashley. *The Cat's Purr*. Atheneum, 1985.

Emberley, Rebecca. *Three Cool Kids*. Little, Brown, 1995.

Hurd, Thacher. *Mystery on the Docks*. Harper, 1983.

Kasza, Keiko. *The Rat and the Tiger*. Putnam, 1993.

Levine, Arthur A. *The Boy Who Drew Cats*. Illustrated by Frederic Clement. Dial, 1993.

O'Brien, Robert C. *Mrs. Frisby and the Rats of NIMH*. Atheneum, 1971.

Ross, Dave, and Dotti Kinzel. *Rat Race and Other Rodent Jokes*. Morrow, 1983.

Sharmat, Marjorie Weinman. *Mooch the Messy*. Illustrated by Ben Shecter. Harper, 1976.

Vaughan, Marcia. *Tingo Tango Mango Tree*. Illustrated by Yvonne Buchanan. Silver Burdett, 1995.

Weiss, Ellen, and Mel Friedman. *The Adventures of Ratman*. Random House, 1990.

THIRTEEN

Rat's Rodent Cousins

Lesson Plan at a Glance

POEM:	"Just for Fun" by J. Patrick Lewis from *A Pet for Me* by Lee Bennett Hopkins
PICTURE BOOK:	*Hannah Mae O'Hannigan's Wild West Show* by Lisa Campbell Ernst
CHAPTER BOOK SELECTION:	*Poppy and Rye* by Avi
POEM:	"The Porcupine" from *Mammalabilia* by Douglas Florian
ORAL TALE:	"Groundhog's Dance" from *Nursery Tales around the World* by Judy Sierra
CHAPTER BOOK SELECTION:	*Ned Mouse Breaks Away* by Tim Wynne-Jones
POEM:	"A Mouse in Her Room"
PICTURE BOOK:	*Moose Tales* by Nancy Van Laan
PICTURE BOOK/READER'S THEATER:	*The Princess Mouse: A Tale from Finland* by Aaron Shepard
ACTIVITY:	The Rodent Best of Show

Preparation and Presentation

This program features mice, hamsters, guinea pigs, gerbils, chipmunks, squirrels, groundhogs, porcupines, beavers, and other members of the rodent family.

Set up a display of nonfiction books that feature not only these animals in the wild, but also pet-care books for the domestic rodents.

POEM

Lewis, J. Patrick. "Just for Fun." In *A Pet for Me*. Edited by Lee Bennett Hopkins. Illustrated by Jane Manning. HarperCollins, 2003.

> This is a good, short ditty to start off the program as the narrator is set to read to his gerbil.

PICTURE BOOK

Ernst, Lisa Campbell. *Hannah Mae O'Hannigan's Wild West Show.* Simon and Schuster, 2003.

> Hannah Mae has always wanted to be a buckaroo. Her trouble is that she lives "smack-dab in the middle of a city where cows were as scarce as a snowball in August." Her parents help her make some city adjustments to horse ridin', ropin', and cow herdin' (by building tiny corrals for hamsters and herding them "from the kitchen to the parlor, from the parlor to the library, and back again"). She finally gets a chance to go out west. When a herd of frightened hamsters runs loose in the open range and scares the real cowboys, Hannah Mae saves the day.

CHAPTER BOOK SELECTION

Avi. *Poppy and Rye.* Avon, 1998.

> Poppy the deer mouse and the unforgettable porcupine Ereth help a bunch of mice face down some encroaching beavers. Read chapter 2, "Poppy and Ereth." Poppy is trying to appeal to Ereth to travel with her. Ereth's dialogue is hilarious and fun to read aloud. Sample phrases include "pickle-tailed fur booger," "frozen frog pips," "twisted bee burp," and "slippery spot of squirrel splat."

POEM

Florian, Douglas. "The Porcupine." In *Mammalabilia*. Harcourt, 2000.

> Hold the book up so that the audience can see the text in the shape of quills along a porcupine's backside. The poem explains why the porcupine is a "porcupain."

ORAL TALE

Sierra, Judy. "Groundhog's Dance." In *Nursery Tales around the World.*
Illustrated by Stefano Vitale. Clarion, 1996.

Seven wolves catch a groundhog in this Cherokee tale. Groundhog teaches
the wolves to dance as a way to celebrate finding good food. He tricks them
with his song. Teach it to the kids ahead of time and let them join in. "Ha
wi ye-a hi, / Ya ha wi ye-a hi, / Ha wi ye-a hi, / Ya ha wi ye-a hi." Before
Groundhog pops into his hole, a wolf bites his tail, and that's why it's been
short ever since.

CHAPTER BOOK SELECTION

Wynne-Jones, Tim. *Ned Mouse Breaks Away.* Groundwood, 2003.

Ned Mouse is sent to jail for writing "The government is unfair to mice" in
his spinach. The rest of the book details Ned's various attempts to escape.
Read chapter 3. Ned makes an extralarge vacuum cleaner in shop and convinces the not-so-bright jail keeper to take the vacuum cleaner to the
Warden's house. The escape plan hilariously backfires. Continue reading
chapter 4. Ned dresses up as a washerwoman and tells the keeper that it's
time for her to go. It takes a few beats for the keeper to realize that the
prison doesn't employ washerwomen. When Ned insults the keeper by
comparing his mental capacity to a gum tree, the keeper smiles and replies
"I like gum."

POEM

"A Mouse in Her Room." Anonymous

> A mouse in her room woke Miss Dowd;
> She was frightened and screamed very loud,
> Then a happy thought hit her—
> To scare off the critter,
> She sat up in bed and meowed.

PICTURE BOOK

Van Laan, Nancy. *Moose Tales.* Illustrated by Amy Rusch. Houghton Mifflin, 1999.

Read the second story, titled "Stuck." Moose bumps into a tree that Beaver
is gnawing. The tree falls on Beaver's tail, trapping him. Moose and the other
woodland animals try to get Beaver free. They gnaw the wood and try to dig

a hole under Beaver to no avail. Moose finally uses his weight to tip one end of the tree up and off Beaver's tail. Have the kids join you for Moose's call for help, "BLAUGGGGGHHHHHHHH!"

PICTURE BOOK/READER'S THEATER

Shepard, Aaron. *The Princess Mouse: A Tale of Finland.* Illustrated by Leonid Gore. Atheneum, 2003.

> According to tradition, when a man wants to marry, he chops down a tree and seeks his sweetheart in the direction the fallen tree points. What happens to Mikko when the only "sweetheart" he finds is a mouse? This little mouse turns out to be a bewitched princess. Read the picture book or have volunteers perform the story as a reader's theater presentation. The script is available on Shepard's web site: www.aaronshep.com. There are parts for eight or more readers.

ACTIVITY

The Rodent Best of Show

> As a follow-up to the "Rats" story theme, invite a local pet store owner to bring in a variety of domestic rodents, such as mice, gerbils, hamsters, and guinea pigs, for the children to pet. You may also wish to announce that kids can bring their own pet rodents. Award each pet a unique award. If you wish, you may simply open the Rodent Best of Show to a more general Pet Best of Show and invite dogs, cats, birds, and reptiles, too.

Mix and Match Picture Books

Alborough, Jez. *Watch Out, Big Bro's Coming!* Candlewick, 1997.

> A frightened mouse yells out to a frog "Help! He's coming! . . . Big Bro . . . He's rough, he's tough, and he's big." The frightened frog warns a parrot, chimpanzee, and an elephant. Big Bro turns out to be the mouse's brother—not so big after all. But he proves that he's rough and tough when the other animals exclaim that he's "teeny-weeny."

Hoberman, Mary Ann. *The Marvelous Mouse Man.* Illustrated by Laura Forman. Harcourt, 2002.

> This is a long but very worthwhile verse retelling of "The Pied Piper of Hamelin" with some twists. A village is overrun by mice and becomes

known as "Mousy Town." The villagers hire a peculiar fellow who leads the mice out of town by waving a scented fan. Afterward, the pets leave, followed by the village children. Things return to normal only when the mice return to town.

Kimmel, Eric. *The Greatest of All.* Illustrated by Giora Carmi. Holiday House, 1991.

Kimmel created a mouse version of the traditional Japanese folktale. Father Mouse's daughter asks permission to wed a handsome field mouse. Her father, however, wishes for a better son-in-law. He asks the human emperor to marry his daughter since the emperor is the greatest of all. The human ruler replies that the Sun is even greater. Father Mouse asks the Sun, Cloud, Wind, and Wall in succession. The Wall says that the greatest of all is the field mouse for his ability to bring down the wall by tunneling underneath. In the end, they all declare, "We mice are the greatest of all." Read the book or tell it as an oral tale.

MacDonald, Amy. *Little Beaver and the Echo.* Illustrated by Sarah Fox-Davies. Putnam, 1990.

Little Beaver cries out, "I'm lonely, I need a friend" across the pond and hears his echo. He sets out to find what he thinks is the voice of another creature looking for a friend. Along the way he meets a duck, an otter, and a turtle—his new friends. Read the echo voice with an echo effect or ask the audience to be the echo.

Ryan, Pam Muñoz. *Mice and Beans.* Illustrated by Joe Cepeda. Scholastic, 2001.

Rosa Maria is an old woman who plans a big celebration for her family. She's determined that no mice will be in the house. She sets mousetraps but finds them missing in the morning. Other items start disappearing, and she distrusts her memory. It turns out that the mice have their own plans. Have the children join in the repeated line, "When it was set and ready to snap, she turned off the light and went to bed."

Schubert, Ingrid, and Dieter Schubert. *Beaver's Lodge.* Front Street, 2001.

Beaver is injured while building his house. Bear and Hedgehog try to finish the job for him. Being a bear and a hedgehog, they are unskilled at building a beaver lodge. The illustration of their final product is a great shot—shell-encrusted mud piles, birdhouses, teddy bears, and more.

Slate, Joseph. *Story Time for Little Porcupine.* Illustrated by Jacqueline Rogers. Marshall Cavendish, 2000.

Through a series of bedtime stories, we learn how porcupines get their quills. When thunderclouds throw down lightning bolts, Big Porcupine in the Sky catches them and attaches them to his back so the bolts won't harm the little porcupines on the ground. The other stories tell how sunsets and stars came to be.

Wisniewski, David. *Sumo Mouse.* Chronicle, 2002.

The cat owner of Tanaka Toys sends his henchmen out to kidnap mice to provide the squeaks for his squeaky toys. Their plans are thwarted by the appearance of superhero Sumo Mouse. The cats think that they've learned Sumo Mouse's secret identity, but they, and the audience, are in for a surprise.

Mix and Match Chapter Book Selections

Avi. *The Mayor of Central Park.* HarperCollins, 2003.

It's the year 1900. Oscar Westerwit, a squirrel, is the unofficial mayor of Central Park, home to mice, chipmunks, voles, and squirrels. Big Daddy Duds, a rat, has plans to take over. Read chapter 12, "Oscar Makes a Discovery." Oscar notices several rats congregating. One of them takes out a pistol and shoots at Oscar, hitting his hat. Continue with chapter 13, "Oscar and the Cop." Oscar reports the shooting to a cop, a bulldog, who informs Oscar that Big Daddy Duds is a pal of the police commissioner.

Jacques, Brian. *Marlfox.* Philomel, 1999.

The eleventh book in the Redwall series is as action packed as the other stories about the woodland creatures of Redwall Abbey and its surroundings. Read the second half of the first chapter. Start with the sentence, "Song plucked a blade of grass and tickled her father's eartip." We meet the squirrel warrior Janglur Swifteye as he confronts two sneaky Marlfoxes. He sends them packing with a dart buried in the nose of one. The chapter ends with the ominous line, "Because we must warn whoever rules at the Abbey that there are Marlfoxes roaming the land."

Levy, Elizabeth. *Night of the Living Gerbil.* HarperCollins, 2001.

Robert's pet gerbil, Exterminator, is dying. Robert is afraid that his weird neighbor is going to turn Exterminator into a zombie. Read chapter 1,

"Ready for the Real Exterminator." Robert's brother makes jokes, for example, "Looks like he's ready for that last ride in the compactor chute to the sky."

Marciano, John Bemelmans. *Harold's Tail*. Viking, 2003.

Harold the squirrel enjoys being the only squirrel in his city park. One day he encounters an unwelcome rat, and the two get into a disagreement about who is better. Read chapter 2, "Please Don't Litter," and chapter 3, "The Broadway Barbershop." The rat convinces Harold to shave his tail. Harold is horrified to learn that without his bushy tail, he looks just like a rat.

Pilkey, Dav. *Ricky Ricotta's Giant Robot vs. the Mutant Mosquitoes from Mercury*. Scholastic, 2000.

Ricky is a mouse who has a huge robot for a friend. Read the very short chapters 1 through 5. When Earth is invaded by Mutant Mosquitoes, it's up to Ricky and his robot to save the day. His teacher, however, won't let him go until he's finished his math problems. The robot speeds up Ricky's grasp of math by using the teachers' cars in the school parking lot as visual aides.

Rylant, Cynthia. *Gooseberry Park*. Harcourt, 1995.

Stumpy is a pregnant squirrel that finds a new tree and makes a nice, clean nest. Read chapter 4. She meets her neighbor Murray, a clumsy bat that has "some problems with his echolocation." When Stumpy asks Murray if he is nocturnal, the bat replies, "No way . . . I'm a Democrat."

Mix and Match Oral Tales

Sierra, Judy. "Magical Mice." In *Silly and Sillier: Read-Aloud Tales from around the World*. Illustrated by Valeri Gorbachev. Knopf, 2002.

A kind old man finds a magical underground kingdom of mice in this Japanese tale. He declares, "May no cats ever disturb your beautiful kingdom." The mice reward his blessing with a magical hammer that produces gold coins every time it strikes. A selfish neighbor learns the story of the hammer and sticks his head down the hole that leads to the mouse kingdom. When he imitates the sound of a cat to make the mice scurry in fear, the hole shrinks around his head, trapping him.

Van Laan, Nancy. "How Beaver Stole Fire." In *In a Circle Long Ago: A Treasury of Native Lore from North America*. Illustrated by Lisa Desimini. Knopf, 1995.

According to this Nez Percé legend, animals and trees talked to each other in the old days. The pine trees have a secret: they have fire. One hard winter, Beaver learns of this secret. When he takes a live coal, the trees chase him. River comes to Beaver's aide and blocks the way with zigzags. Beaver shares the secret of fire with other trees. "Now all who wanted fire would be told how to rub willow and birch and other sticks together in a special way. They would be able to create a fire of their own."

Mix and Match Poetry

Dahl, Roald. "The Porcupine." In *Dirty Beasts*. Illustrated by Quentin Blake. Farrar, Straus and Giroux, 1983.

Dotlich, Rebecca Kai. "Porcupine." In *Hoofbeats, Claws and Rippled Fins: Creature Poems*. Edited by Lee Bennett Hopkins. Illustrated by Stephen Alcorn. HarperCollins, 2002.

Eastwick, Ivy O. "Mice's Song." In *Some Folks Like Cats and Other Poems*. Illustrated by Mary Kurnick Maass. Boyds Mill, 2002.

Gardner, John. "The Flying Squirrel." In *Eric Carle's Animals, Animals*. Edited and illustrated by Eric Carle. Philomel, 1989.

George, Kristine O'Connell. "Breakfast." In *Toasting Marshmallows: Camping Poems*. Illustrated by Kate Kiesler. Clarion, 2001.

Harley, Avis. "Hamster Hide-and-Seek." In *A Pet for Me*. Edited by Lee Bennett Hopkins. Illustrated by Jane Manning. HarperCollins, 2003.

Hoberman, Mary Ann. "Mouse." In *The Llama Who Had No Pajama*. Illustrated by Betty Fraser. Harcourt, 1998.

Howcraft, Wilbur G. "The Personable Porcupine." In *A Zooful of Animals*. Edited by William Cole. Illustrated by Lynn Munsinger. Houghton Mifflin, 1992.

Kennedy, X. J. "Who to Pet and Who Not to Pet." In *Exploding Gravy: Poems to Make You Laugh*. Illustrated by Joy Allen. Little, Brown, 2002.

Kuskin, Karla. "The Porcupine." In *Eric Carle's Animals, Animals*. Edited and illustrated by Eric Carle. Philomel, 1989.

Lewis, J. Patrick. "Just Fur Fun." In *A Pet for Me*. Edited by Lee Bennett Hopkins. Illustrated by Jane Manning. HarperCollins, 2003.

Luton, Mildred. "The Mouse Ate the Bait." In *A Zooful of Animals*. Edited by William Cole. Illustrated by Lynn Munsinger. Houghton Mifflin, 1992.

Prelutsky, Jack. "Boing! Boing! Squeak!" and "Nice Mice." In *The New Kid on the Block*. Illustrated by James Stevenson. Greenwillow, 1984.

———. "Chipmunk, Chipmunk," "I've Got a Three-Thousand-Pound Cat," "My Gerbil Seems Bedraggled," and "An Unobservant Porcupine." In *A Pizza the Size of the Sun*. Illustrated by James Stevenson. Greenwillow, 1996.

———. "The House Mouse." In *Read-Aloud Rhymes for the Very Young*. Illustrated by Marc Brown. Knopf, 1986.

———. "In Minot, North Dakota." In *The Frogs Wore Red Suspenders*. Illustrated by Petra Mathers. Greenwillow, 2002.

Singer, Marilyn. "Beavers in November" and "Deer Mouse." In *Turtle in July*. Illustrated by Jerry Pinkney. Macmillan, 1989.

Tweaking the Program Theme . . .

. . . For Preschoolers

Drop the Shepard reader's theater/picture book and one of the two chapter book selections, and substitute the following picture books:

Emberley, Ed. *Thanks, Mom*. Little, Brown, 2003.

> This cumulative story is set in a circus. Kiko the mouse sees a piece of cheese. Gato the cat chases Kiko, Fido the dog chases Gato, Otto the tiger chases Fido, Mumbo the elephant chases Otto, and Koko, Kiko's mother, winds up chasing Mumbo. The kids will chant the refrain "Run, Kiko, Run! / But don't drop that delicious cheese!"

Shea, Pegi Deitz, and Cynthia Weill. *Ten Mice for Tet*. Illustrated by To Ngoc Trang. Embroidery by Pham Viet Dinh. Chronicle, 2003.

> This counting book follows a group of mice preparing for the Vietnamese new year, Tet. They are depicted following traditional steps of preparation for the celebration. The illustrations are a fascinating combination of embroidery and drawings.

. . . For Fifth and Sixth Graders

Drop the Ernst and Van Laan picture books, and substitute the following:

MacDonald, Margaret Read. "Two Women Hunt for Ground Squirrels." In *Earth Care: World Folktales to Talk About*. Linnet, 1999.

Tell this oral Tanaha Athabaskan tale about the harm humans cause when they slaughter young animals. A woman catches a ground squirrel child. She then ends up in a ground squirrel house. The huntress finds a ground squirrel mother singing to her suffering child. The human learns that her snare has harmed the ground squirrel child. The huntress learns her lesson and returns to her meadow.

Thurber, James. "The Scotty Who Knew Too Much." In *The Thurber Carnival*. Harper, 1945.

A tough little Scotty visits the country and hears about a cat with a black and white stripe. He fights it and winds up on his back. He next hears about a strange animal with quills. He fights that creature and is knocked out. He later tells a farm dog that the strange creature pulled a knife on him. The tough Scotty fights the farm dog but is too distracted from defending himself against smells and knives that he, once again, is badly beaten. Thurber ends his wry humorous fable with the moral, "It is better to ask some questions than to know all the answers."

And Yet Even More Titles about Mice, Gerbils, Hamsters, Guinea Pigs, Squirrels, Groundhogs, Porcupines, Beavers, and other Rodent Cousins of Rat for You to Consider

Asch, Frank. *Class Pets: Battle in a Bottle*. Simon and Schuster, 2003.

Banks, Lynn Reid. *I, Houdini: The Amazing Story of an Escape-Artist Hamster*. Doubleday, 1978.

Bond, Michael. *The Tales of Olga da Polga*. Macmillan, 1971.

Cleary, Beverly. *The Mouse and the Motorcycle*. Morrow, 1965.

Kesey, Ken. *Little Tricker the Squirrel Meets Big Double the Bear*. Illustrated by Barry Moser. Viking, 1990.

King-Smith, Dick. *Jenius: The Amazing Guinea Pig*. Illustrated by Brian Floca. Hyperion, 1996.

———. *Magnus Powermouse*. HarperCollins, 1984.

Korman, Susan. *Groundhog at Evergreen Road.* Illustrated by Higgins Bond. Soundprints, 2003.

Lawson, Robert. *Ben and Me.* Little, Brown, 1939.

Lester, Helen. *A Porcupine Named Fluffy.* Illustrated by Lynn Munsinger. Houghton Mifflin, 1986.

Lithgow, John. *Micawber.* Illustrated by C. F. Payne. Simon and Schuster, 2001.

Ripper, George. *Brian and Bob: The Tale of Two Guinea Pigs.* Hyperion, 2003.

Rylant, Cynthia. *Thimbleberry Stories.* Illustrated by Maggie Kneen. Harcourt, 2000.

Steig, William. *Able's Island.* Farrar, Straus and Giroux, 1976.

Stevenson, James. *The Castaway.* Greenwillow, 2002.

Waddell, Martin. *Sam Vole and His Brothers.* Illustrated by Barbara Firth. Candlewick, 1992.

———. *Squeak-a-Lot.* Illustrated by Virginia Miller. Greenwillow, 1991.

Wolf, Jake. *What You Do Is Easy, What I Do Is Hard.* Illustrated by Anna Dewdney. Greenwillow, 1996.

Yep, Laurence. *The Curse of the Squirrel.* Random House, 1987.

FOURTEEN

Down and Dirty

Lesson Plan at a Glance

Song: "Mud" from the recording *Summersongs* by John McCutcheon

Picture Book: *Preschool to the Rescue* by Judy Sierra

Picture Book: *Diary of a Worm* by Doreen Cronin

Chapter Book Selection: *Junie B. Jones Smells Something Fishy* by Barbara Park

Poem: "Burrows" from *Footprints on the Roof: Poems about the Earth* by Marilyn Singer

Picture Book: *Earthquack!* by Margie Palatini

Chapter Book Selection: *Danger in Quicksand Swamp* by Bill Wallace

Poem: "Captain Hook" from *Where the Sidewalk Ends* by Shel Silverstein

Oral Tale: "Todo O Nada" from *Celebrate the World: Twenty Tellable Folktales for Multicultural Festivals* by Margaret Read MacDonald

Activity: Treasure Hunt in the Library

Preparation and Presentation

This theme covers many different aspects of being "down" (the creatures who live down below) and "dirty" (messy), capped off with a buried-treasure focus.

SONG

McCutcheon, John. "Mud." In *Summersongs* (recording). Rounder, 1995.

> Play this song as the audience enters the program area. While waiting for the show to begin, they will find themselves chanting along with the catchy chorus, "covered with, covered with mud, mud . . ."

PICTURE BOOK

Sierra, Judy. *Preschool to the Rescue*. Illustrated by Will Hillenbrand. Harcourt, 2001.

> A sleepy, creepy mud puddle traps a pizza truck, a police car, a tow truck, a backhoe, and a fire engine before being rescued by a class of preschoolers. The vehicles turn out to be toys. Even though the book features preschoolers, the elementary-age crowd will also enjoy this fun story.

PICTURE BOOK

Cronin, Doreen. *Diary of a Worm*. Illustrated by Harry Bliss. Joanna Cotler, 2003.

> A young worm shares his daily journal, which includes trying to teach a spider to dig, avoiding girls who play hopscotch, insulting his sister, and doing the hokey pokey. "You put your head in. You put your head out. You do the hokey pokey and you turn yourself about. That's all we could do."

CHAPTER BOOK SELECTION

Park, Barbara. *Junie B. Jones Smells Something Fishy*. Random House, 1998.

> Junie B. is upset when she learns that she cannot take her dog to school for Pet Day. Grandma Miller helps her find a pet earthworm, which Junie B. names Noodle. Read chapter 5, "Catching Friends." Junie B. adds an injured fly and a bunch of ants to Noodle's jar.

POEM

Singer, Marilyn. "Burrows." In *Footprints on the Roof: Poems about the Earth*. Illustrated by Meilo So. Knopf, 2002.

> The poem describes the "mazy metropolis" that humans never see. The narrator treads softly, "a quiet giant leaving only footprints on the roof." Other good poems from this collection, which fit the program theme, include "Caves" and "Mud."

PICTURE BOOK

Palatini, Margie. *Earthquack!* Illustrated by Barry Moser. Simon and Schuster, 2002.

Chucky Ducky, Lucy Goosie, Brewster Rooster, Sue Ewe and her lambs, Nanny Goat and Billy the kid, Merle the Squirrel, Iggy Piggy, and Vickie, Nickie, and Rickie Chickie are worried about a series of rumbles. Along the way, they foil the evil attempts of a weasel. The quakes turn out to be Joel and Lowell Mole looking for their cousin underground and asking, "Does anyone know the way to San Jose?"

CHAPTER BOOK SELECTION

Wallace, Bill. *Danger in Quicksand Swamp.* Holiday House, 1989.

This action-packed story describes the attempts of two boys to locate a buried treasure on an island in the middle of a swamp. The boys face mosquitoes, quicksand, alligators, and a mystery man who is trying to kill them. Read chapter 15. Jake is in the water with an alligator close behind. Although Jake makes it onto the island, so does the alligator. The chapter ends with the cliff-hanging line, "There was more than one alligator!"

POEM

Silverstein, Shel. "Captain Hook." In *Where the Sidewalk Ends.* HarperCollins, 1974.

The kids might already be familiar with this funny poem about a pirate from what is perhaps the most popular children's poetry book of all time. It fits in nicely with the buried treasure aspect of the theme.

ORAL TALE

MacDonald, Margaret Read. "Todo O Nada." In *Celebrate the World: Twenty Tellable Folktales for Multicultural Festivals.* Wilson, 1994.

Poor farmer Cesario Balderas finds a treasure of gold in a mysterious cave. A loud voice thunders, "TODO O NADA! All . . . or Nothing!" Cesario fails to lift the entire treasure, so he leaves empty-handed. When he returns, he cannot find the cave. No one has ever found it since. MacDonald does a wonderful job of giving tips to telling this fun lead-in to the final "Treasure Hunt in the Library" activity.

ACTIVITY

Treasure Hunt in the Library

Make a crude facsimile of a pirate's treasure map ahead of time. It should show the various parts of the library as they might appear on a treasure island. For example, drinking fountains can be labeled on the map as waterfalls. Shelves and aisles could be labeled as cliffs and ravines. A plant can be represented on the map as a tree. Stuffed animals or puppets can be placed around the library to represent wildlife refuges. Count the number of paces it takes from your program area (the starting place) to the "buried treasure," represented by "X marks the spot" on the map. The treasure can be an assortment of candy, stickers, and other treats. We've had fun crawling on our hands and knees past the reference desk (the "pirate ship") to "avoid being seen" (and to the great amusement of staff, parents, and other library patrons watching the fun).

Mix and Match Picture Books

Becker, Bonny. *An Ant's Day Off*. Illustrated by Nina Laden. Simon and Schuster, 2003.

Never in the history of "antdom" has an ant taken a day off work. Nonetheless, Bart, who has spent his entire life underground, wants to view the world above. There's a hilarious encounter with two frogs chanting the "Row, Row, Row Your Boat" song.

Dr. Seuss. *Yertle the Turtle and Other Stories*. Random House, 1958.

Read the last story, titled "The Big Brag." A bear, who brags how far he can smell, and a rabbit, who brags how far he can hear, are both upstaged by a tiny worm, who sees so far that he sees all the way around the world to find "the two biggest fools that have ever been seen." The story was also reprinted in the now out-of-print Seuss picture book:

The Big Brag. Random House, 1998.

Ehlert, Lois. *Mole's Hill*. Harcourt, 1994.

This picture book, inspired by a Seneca tale, features a mole that digs tunnels and creates a home out of a hill. Fox demands that the hill be removed. Mole comes up with a clever plan to save her home.

Harley, Bill. *Sarah's Story*. Illustrated by Eve Aldridge. Tricycle, 1996.

Sarah has an underground adventure inside an ant colony and a beehive. The story can also be found on the following Harley recording:

Come On Out and Play. Round River Records, 1990. Check out Harley's web site to purchase the recording: www.billharley.com.

Head, Judith. *Mud Soup*. Illustrated by Susan Guevara. Random House, 2003.

Rosa and her *abuela* (grandmother) jokingly refer to their black bean soup as "Mud Soup." Rosa's friend Josh mistakenly believes the soup is actually made of mud and frets about tasting it.

MacDonald, Betty. *Mrs. Piggle-Wiggle*. Lippincott, 1947.

Tell or read the chapter "The Radish Cure," in which a girl named Patsy refuses to take a bath until her parents apply Mrs. Piggle-Wiggle's unorthodox solution. The story was also featured in MacDonald's now out-of-print picture book:

Mrs. Piggle-Wiggle's Won't-Take-a-Bath Cure. Illustrated by Bruce Whatley. HarperCollins, 1997.

MacDonald, Margaret Read. *Slop! A Welsh Folktale*. Illustrated by Yvonne LeBrun Davis. Fulcrum Kids, 1997.

An old man and an old woman throw the contents of their slop bucket over the front garden wall every evening until one night a tiny voice yells at them to stop. The slops have been entering the house of a wee little family through their chimney. The story can also be found in the following MacDonald collection:

Peace Tales. Linnet, 1992.

Palatini, Margie. *Tub-Boo-Boo*. Illustrated by Glin Dibley. Simon and Schuster, 2001.

Henry makes a "tub-boo-boo" when his big toe gets stuck in the spigot. In an unlikely chain of events, his mother gets her fingers stuck in the spigot, followed by his father, who gets his tie stuck, and a policeman, who also gets his finger stuck. After a plumber is unsuccessful in freeing everyone, Lucy Hathaway saves the day with her Chocolate Chunky Chip ice cream.

Wheeler, Lisa. *One Dark Night*. Illustrated by Ivan Bates. Harcourt, 2003.

A wee little mouse and a mole live in a hole. They leave their home and encounter a very hungry bear. This is a fun story full of alliteration. Pause before the punch line, "You're late!" Use a wee little voice for the mouse and mole segments and a deep voice for the bear's parts.

Mix and Match Chapter Book Selections

Bunting, Eve. *Nasty, Stinky Sneakers.* HarperCollins, 1994.

If Colin wins the Stinkiest Sneakers in the World Contest, he'll win three pairs of brand-new sneakers. Read chapter 2. Colin shares his game plan for the creation of his foul-smelling sneakers. His tactics include "No washing of feet" and "Sleeping with your sneakers on." The chapter ends with Colin discovering his nasty creation is missing.

Naylor, Phyllis Reynolds. *The Treasure of Bessledorf Hill.* Atheneum, 1997.

Did the pirate Peg Leg really bury a treasure on Bessledorf Hill? Read chapter 8, "Peg Leg." Bernie, Georgene, and Weasel discover that someone—perhaps Peg Leg himself—has dug a series of holes in the middle of the night.

Sachar, Louis. *Holes.* Farrar, Straus and Giroux, 1998.

Read chapter 7. Stanley digs his first hole. Even though the beauty of this Newbery Award–winning book is in the interweaving of the different story lines, for the purposes of this program, limit your reading to the sections on Stanley (skip the Madame Zeroni story line). This will give the audience a sense of the hopelessness of Stanley's situation.

Scieszka, Jon. *The Not-So-Jolly Roger.* Viking, 1991.

The Time Warp Trio travels back in time to witness the pirate Blackbeard bury his treasure on a deserted island. Read chapter 3. The boys learn that the mean pirate is "not the Disney version" when they see him murder his two shipmates. The chapter ends with Blackbeard catching sight of the boys, raising his pistols, and firing.

Sobol, Donald J. *Encyclopedia Brown and the Case of the Disgusting Sneakers.* Morrow, 1990.

Read the chapter "The Case of Black Jack's Treasure." A con man promises to show folks where Black Jack buried his treasure. Encyclopedia Brown cleverly exposes the con man. Ask the audience members how Brown solved the case. The answer can be found at the back of the book.

Mix and Match Poetry

Armour, Joyce. "Icky." In *Kids Pick the Funniest Poems*. Edited by Bruce Lansky. Illustrated by Stephen Carpenter. Meadowbrook, 1991.

Bagert, Brod. "Booger Love." In *Giant Children*. Illustrated by Tedd Arnold. Dial, 2002.

Bergengren, Ralph. "The Worm." In *Never Take a Pig to Lunch: And Other Poems about the Fun of Eating*. Edited and illustrated by Nadine Bernard Westcott. Orchard, 1994.

Chaikin, Miriam. "A Blade of Grass." In *Don't Step on the Sky: A Handful of Haiku*. Illustrated by Hiroe Nakata. Holt, 2002.

Dodds, Bill. "Molly Peters." In *A Bad Case of the Giggles*. Edited by Bruce Lansky. Illustrated by Stephen Carpenter. Meadowbrook, 1994.

Florian, Douglas. "I'm in the Mood for Mud." In *Bing Bang Boing*. Harcourt, 1994.

———. "Pig Out." In *Laugh-eteria*. Harcourt, 1999.

Giovanni, Nikki. "trips." In *Spin a Soft Black Song*. Rev. ed. Illustrated by George Martins. Hill and Wang, 1985.

Hoberman, Mary Ann. "The Puppy." In *You Read to Me, I'll Read to You*. Illustrated by Michael Emberley. Little, Brown, 2001.

Hubbell, Patricia. "The Vacuum Cleaner's Revenge." In *Dirty Laundry Pile: Poems in Different Voices*. Edited by Paul Janeczko. Illustrated by Melissa Sweet. HarperCollins, 2001.

Katz, Bobbi. "Washing Machine." In *Dirty Laundry Pile: Poems in Different Voices*. Edited by Paul Janeczko. Illustrated by Melissa Sweet. HarperCollins, 2001.

Lansky, Bruce. "Oops!" In *If Pigs Could Fly and Other Deep Thoughts*. Illustrated by Stephen Carpenter. Meadowbrook, 2000.

Lee, Dennis. "The Muddy Puddle." In *The Random House Book of Poetry for Children*. Edited by Jack Prelutsky. Illustrated by Arnold Lobel. Random House, 1983.

Lewis, J. Patrick. "The Hippopotamole." In *The Bookworm's Feast: A Potluck of Poems*. Illustrated by John O'Brien. Dial, 1999.

Philip, Neil. "Dirt Has Its Uses, Too." In *The Fish Is Me: Bathtime Rhymes*. Illustrated by Claire Henley. Clarion, 2002.

Prelutsky, Jack. "Dainty Dottie Dee." In *The New Kid on the Block*. Illustrated by James Stevenson. Greenwillow, 1984.

———. "An Early Worm Got out of Bed" and "Mold, Mold." In *Something Big Has Been Here*. Illustrated by James Stevenson. Greenwillow, 1990.

Schertle, Alice. "Invitation from a Mole." In *A Lucky Thing*. Illustrated by Wendell Minor. Harcourt, 1999.

Singer, Marilyn. "Ants" and "Mole." In *Fireflies at Midnight*. Illustrated by Ken Robbins. Atheneum, 2003.

Snyder, Zilpha Keatly. "Poem to Mud." In *The Twentieth Century Children's Poetry Treasury*. Edited by Jack Prelutsky. Illustrated by Meilo So. Knopf, 1999.

Steig, Jeanne. "The Mole." In *Beauty of the Beast: Poems from the Animal Kingdom*. Edited by Jack Prelutsky. Illustrated by Meilo So. Knopf, 1997.

Stewart, Don. "Recipe for Making Mud Pies." In *Kids Pick the Funniest Poems*. Edited by Bruce Lansky. Illustrated by Stephen Carpenter. Meadowbrook, 1991.

Tweaking the Program Theme . . .

. . . *For Preschoolers*

Drop the MacDonald oral story, the Palatini picture book, the Singer poem, and the Wallace chapter book selection, and replace them with the following picture books:

Krensky, Stephen. *What a Mess!* Illustrated by Joe Mathieu. Random House, 2001.

There's mud on the rug. Who made this mess? The kids each deny that they made the mess (all the while making their own messes). In the end, the culprit turns out to be Dad.

Root, Phyllis. *One Duck Stuck*. Illustrated by Jane Chapman. Candlewick, 1998.

Duck is stuck in the muck and needs two fish, three moose, four crickets, five frogs, six skunks, seven snails, eight possums, nine snakes, and ten dragonflies to "un-splunk" him.

Zimmerman, Andrea, and David Clemesha. *Digger Man*. Holt, 2003.

A little boy fantasizes driving his own life-size digger to scoop up rocks, push mud, dig holes, and make big hills.

Zimmerman, Andrea, and David Clemesha. *Trashy Town.* Illustrated by Dan Yaccarino. HarperCollins, 1999.

> Mr. Gilly, the trashman, adds more and more trash to his big trash truck. The kids will soon answer the refrain, "Is the trash truck full yet?" with a loud "No!"

. . . For Fifth and Sixth Graders

Drop the Park chapter book selection and the Sierra picture book, and substitute the following books:

Feiffer, Jules. *By the Side of the Road.* Hyperion, 2002.

> This is a cross between a picture book and a graphic novel. The story is about a stubborn boy and his equally stubborn father, who leaves him by the side of the road for misbehaving. The boy grows to like it there and, as he grows older, creates an underground community. Older kids will enjoy this absurd tale. Ask them what type of dwelling they would create if left to their own resources.

Macaulay, David. *Underground.* Houghton Mifflin, 1976.

> Leave this book out for perusal after the program is over. The imaginative drawings show a cross section of the underground man-made structures below a city's surface.

And Yet Even More Down and Dirty Titles for You to Consider

Cleary, Beverly. *The Real Hole.* Illustrated by Dyanne DiSalvo Ryan. Morrow, 1986.

Lewis, Kevin. *My Truck Is Stuck.* Illustrated by Dan Kirk. Hyperion, 2002.

Munsch, Robert. *Mud Puddle.* Rev. ed. Illustrated by Sami Suomalainen. Annick, 1995.

Plourde, Lynn. *Pigs in the Mud in the Middle of the Rud.* Illustrated by John Schoenherr. Blue Sky, 1997.

Pomerantz, Charlotte. *The Piggy in the Puddle.* Illustrated by James Marshall. Macmillan, 1974.

Yolen, Jane. *Eeny, Meeny, Miney, Mole.* Illustrated by Kathryn Brown. Harcourt, 1992.

Zion, Gene. *Harry, the Dirty Dog.* Illustrated by Margaret Bloy Graham. Harper, 1956.

FIFTEEN

What Stinks?

Lesson Plan at a Glance

OPENING ACTIVITY: Riddles and Poems about Skunks

PICTURE BOOK: *Sweet Briar Goes to School* by
Karma Wilson

SONG: "Stinky, Stinky, Diaper Change" from *Take Me Out of the Bathtub and Other Silly Dilly Songs* by Alan Katz

PICTURE BOOK: *The Stinky Cheese Man and Other Fairly Stupid Tales* by Jon Scieszka

POEM: "The Perfect Couple" from *The Burger and the Hot Dog* by Jim Aylesworth

CHAPTER BOOK SELECTION: "The Stinky Princess" from *Odder Than Ever* by Bruce Coville

ORAL STORY: "Little Snot Nose Boy" from *Celebrate the World: Twenty Tellable Folktales for Multicultural Festivals* by Margaret Read MacDonald

POEM: "Dirty Socks" from *If Pigs Could Fly and Other Deep Thoughts* by Bruce Lansky

SONG: "Black Socks"

POEM:	"What the Garbage Truck Ate for Breakfast Today" from *Bing Bang Boing* by Douglas Florian
PICTURE BOOK/ACTIVITY:	*I Stink!* by Kate McMullan
ACTIVITY:	Experiments from *Science Fair Success with Scents, Aromas, and Smells* by Thomas R. Rybolt and Leah M. Rybolt

Preparation and Presentation

This program features the wonderful world of odor (mostly bad odors), noses, and the various things that cause those distinct smells. This theme works well in conjunction with the "Chapter 14: Down and Dirty" program theme in this book. Many of the materials and ideas can be swapped between the two themes.

OPENING ACTIVITY

Riddles and Poems about Skunks

Here are a few "rotten" riddles to set the tone for the program:

Q: What did the judge say when the skunk came into the courtroom?
A: Odor in the court!

Q: What does a skunk do when it's angry?
A: It raises a stink.

Q: What's black and white and red all over?
A: A skunk with diaper rash.

Q: What do you get when you cross a fairy with a skunk?
A: Stinkerbell.

Q: What do you get when you cross a bear with a skunk?
A: Winnie the Pooh.

PICTURE BOOK

Wilson, Karma. *Sweet Briar Goes to School.* Illustrated by LeUyen Pham. Dial, 2003.

A little skunk's new classmates tease her for being a skunk. They call her rotten and smelly and hold their noses while exclaiming "EEW!" After a wolf grabs one of the students during recess, Sweet Briar saves the day when she remembers her mama's rule, "To keep the wolves and bears away, lift your tail and spray, spray, spray!"

SONG

Katz, Alan. "Stinky, Stinky, Diaper Change." In *Take Me Out of the Bathtub and Other Silly Dilly Songs*. Illustrated by David Catrow. Margaret K. McElderry, 2001.

The narrator complains about the strange odor coming from his or her baby brother to the tune of "Twinkle, Twinkle, Little Star." Other songs from this collection that fit this and the "Down and Dirty" program theme include "I'm Filthy, I'm Dirty" (tune of "It's Raining, It's Pouring"), "The Yogurt Flies Straight from My Brother" (tune of "My Bonnie Lies over the Ocean"), "I've Been Cleaning Up My Bedroom" (tune of "I've Been Working on the Railroad"), and the book's title song (tune of "Take Me Out to the Ball Game").

PICTURE BOOK

Scieszka, Jon. *The Stinky Cheese Man and Other Fairly Stupid Tales*. Illustrated by Lane Smith. Viking, 1992.

Read the title story from this extremely popular book. For those two children's librarians not familiar with the story, it's a takeoff of the traditional story, "The Gingerbread Man." In Scieszka's version, no one wants to chase the Stinky Cheese Man because of his pungent smell. The illustration of the cow's reaction to the main character is priceless.

POEM

Aylesworth, Jim. "The Perfect Couple." In *The Burger and the Hot Dog*. Illustrated by Stephen Gammell. Atheneum, 2001.

This is a good companion piece to Scieszka's *The Stinky Cheese Man and Other Fairly Stupid Tales* picture book. This narrative poem is about a wedge of cheese named Woodrow that is sad because folks yell out, "pee-you." He falls in love with Wanda, "a pungent wedge as well."

CHAPTER BOOK SELECTION

Coville, Bruce. "The Stinky Princess." In *Odder Than Ever*. Harcourt, 1999.

Read the first part of this short story, which starts with the captivating line, "Once there was a princess named Violet who didn't smell very good."

Violet hangs out with a goblin and starts to acquire some of his smell. She runs away from home. The goblin tries to return her, but the king is so offended by the smell that he refuses to allow her back. Coville penned these powerful lines, "It is, after all, one thing to run away from home. It is another thing entirely to run away and discover that they don't want you back." Read the first half of the story up to the point where the king and his army ride away and Violet goes to the goblin's home.

ORAL STORY

MacDonald, Margaret Read. "Little Snot Nose Boy." In *Celebrate the World: Twenty Tellable Folktales for Multicultural Festivals.* Wilson, 1994.

This Japanese folktale is similar to the Brothers Grimm tale "The Fisherman and His Wife." A poor person gets wish after wish but eventually loses everything by being too greedy. In this version, the wishes are granted by the snot-nosed boy, who blows his nose three times to make the wishes come true. MacDonald gives some very helpful tips and encourages the teller to be uninhibited and let loose with guttural blowing noises and wiping of sleeves under the nose.

POEM

Lansky, Bruce. "Dirty Socks." In *If Pigs Could Fly and Other Deep Thoughts.* Illustrated by Stephen Carpenter. Meadowbrook, 2000.

A local lake gets polluted after someone washes their disgusting socks in it. Pair this poem with the following song.

SONG

"Black Socks." Anonymous

Sing this traditional camp favorite either solo or print the words for everyone to see and lead them singing it as a round.

> "Black socks, they never need washing,
> The longer you wear them the stronger they get.
> Sometimes I think I should change them,
> But something inside me keeps saying
> Not yet, not yet, not yet . . ."

To learn the tune, check out the following recording:

Harley, Bill. *Monsters in the Bathroom.* Round River, 1984. You can purchase the recording from www.billharley.com.

POEM

Florian, Douglas. "What the Garbage Truck Ate for Breakfast Today." In *Bing Bang Boing.* Harcourt, 1994.

This litany of disgusting items, including dirty diapers, is a nice companion piece to the following picture book.

PICTURE BOOK/ACTIVITY

McMullan, Kate. *I Stink!* Illustrated by Jim McMullan. HarperCollins, 2002.

This book is great to read aloud in a raucous character voice. An anthropomorphic garbage truck brags to the reader about his importance in hauling trash away. He's rude ("Did I wake you? Too bad!") and funny ("No skunk ever stunk this bad"). The audience will automatically register their disgust at the alphabetical litany of garbage, such as *D* for "dirty diapers" and *P* for "puppy poo."

After the story is read, brainstorm with the audience for more examples of alphabetical garbage items, such as *S* for "spoiled spinach." Write them on a board or large tablet for all to see. Provide paper and drawing materials for the audience, and let them pick and choose which disgusting objects they would like to draw. Use Jim McMullan's illustrations as a model. The use of the color green drawn in wavy lines goes a long way in creating the impression of bad smells emanating from those items. After the kids have finished their drawings, reread the alphabet section of the book again (in your garbage-truck voice), with the audience holding up the new drawings at the appropriate times.

ACTIVITY

Rybolt, Thomas R., and Leah M. Rybolt. *Science Fair Success with Scents, Aromas, and Smells.* Enslow, 2002.

Experiment "1.3 Location by Nose" is a nice, simple wrap-up activity for the program. Bring ten index cards. Before the program starts, put a little peppermint extract on one side of one card and place a pencil mark on it. Bring the index cards out during the program and lay them on a table (with the pencil mark facedown). Let the audience members try to locate the correct card with their nose. Try different odors. Check out the book for more detailed instructions and dozens of other simple experiments involving both good and bad scents. End the program with a treat that has a pleasant odor, such as peppermints or popcorn. Another science experiment book that features a chapter devoted to "Stinky Science" is

> Parker, Steve. *Shocking, Slimy, Stinky, Shiny Science Experiments.* Sterling, 1998.

Mix and Match Picture Books

De Groat, Diane. *Roses Are Pink, Your Feet Really Stink.* Morrow, 1996.

Although there are no actual odors present in this book, Gilbert's attitude stinks when he writes nasty valentines to two not-so-nice classmates. One of the cards reads, "Violets are blue / Roses are pink / Your feet are big / And they really stink." To top it off, Gilbert signs the two classmate's names on each other's card.

Freymann, Saxton, and Joost Eiffers. *Dr. Pompo's Nose.* Scholastic, 2000.

This is a weird, yet fun, story that accompanies color photographs of pumpkins with humanlike faces (but not jack-o'-lanterns). The characters find a pumpkin stem but aren't sure what it is. Guesses include a tool for gardening, a horn for calling sheep, a listening device, and a fossil. The pumpkin Ms. Sniffen claims that it is her nose and asks Dr. Pompo to attach it back. He does but inverts it. Have fun reading Ms. Sniffen's nose-affected lines, such as "Help me wid by doze!"

Greenberg, David T. *Skunks!* Illustrated by Lynn Munsinger. Little, Brown, 2001.

This is an ode to the stink of skunks. One can use their spray to get rid of insects, propel hovercrafts, and wash windows. Skunks also make excellent hats, slippers, and bed comforters. Use a skunk puppet to imitate the many times skunks spray their intended targets in this book.

Kajikawa, Kimiko. *Yoshi's Feast.* Illustrated by Yumi Heo. DK, 2000.

Yoshi enjoys the smells of Sabu's broiled eels but is too cheap to purchase any in this adaptation of a Japanese folktale. Sabu angrily presents Yoshi a bill for smelling the eels. Yoshi retaliates by paying the amount in the sound of coins jingling. The two cleverly work out their differences in the end.

Keillor, Garrison. *The Old Man Who Loved Cheese.* Illustrated by Anne Wilsdorf. Little, Brown, 1996.

> A man named Wallace P. Flynn has a fondness for really strong-smelling cheese: "Cheese that smelled like socks from a marathon race."

Schwarz, Viviane. *The Adventures of a Nose.* Illustrated by Joel Stewart. Candlewick, 2002.

> A nose wanders around the world looking for "a place where I can fit in." Hold the pictures up so all can see that the nose fits perfectly in several scenarios. See how long it takes for your audience to catch the visual "gimmick" of the book.

Weiss, Ellen. *The Nose Knows.* Illustrated by Margeaux Lucas. Kane, 2002.

> Peter, "The Family Nose," uses his super sense of smell to ferret out the rotting broccoli from his brother's closet, the swampy smell coming from a flower vase, and the deadly smell of rotten eggs that signals a gas leak. In the end, "The Family Nose" becomes "The Family Stuffed Nose."

Mix and Match Chapter Book Selections

Danziger, Paula. *Amber Brown Sees Red.* Putnam, 1997.

> Amber's school is faced with a skunk problem. Read the second and third chapters. While some kids make fun of the skunk odor by lifting their legs and pretending to spray, other students become sick and afraid.

Howe, James. *The Odorous Adventures of Stinky Dog.* Atheneum, 2003.

> Howie the dachshund creates a story about Stinky Dog, a superhero canine who solves problems with his super stench. Read chapter 6, "Making the World Safe for Stinkiness." Stinky Dog and his crime-fighting sidekick Little D (a sparrow) sew superhero outfits (with a nod to Martha Stewart) and learn news about their archnemesis, B-Man (which stands for Bath Man).

McKenna, Colleen O'Shaughnessy. *Third Grade Stinks!* Holiday House, 2001.

> Gordie and Lucy do not like each other, and both are dismayed when their teacher forces them to share a locker. Read chapter 6. Gordie and his friend Lamont plot to "stink her out" of the locker with sardines.

Preller, James. *The Case of the Stinky Science Project*. Scholastic, 2000.

> The kids make a volcano for the class science fair, but when the lava spews out, it not only spews extra bubbles, but also a horrible stench. Read the brief chapters 9 and 10, which both sum up the story and solve the mystery.

Torrey, Michele. *The Case of the Gasping Garbage*. Dutton, 2001.

> Doyle and Fossey are young Science Detectives who help solve the mystery of the weird noises coming from the garbage can. One person thinks it might be a monster, but then the smell of baked bread emanates from the can. Read the chapters "Monster Mission" and "Great Gasping Garbage." These two chapters make up the entire title story in this collection of short mysteries.

Mix and Match Oral Tale

DeSpain, Pleasant. "The Big, Smelly, Hairy Toe." In *Sweet Land of Story: Thirty-Six American Tales to Tell*. August House, 2000.

> This Appalachian folktale is similar to the popular legend "Tailypo." A man finds a "giant, smelly, hairy toe buried in a muddy hole." He throws it in a stew and gobbles it down, which is sure to elicit groans from the audience. A voice hollers, "Who, oh who, has my big, smelly, hairy toe?" There are some funny lines mixed in this scary story, such as when the man replies, "Two of my toes are big, and some of them are smelly."

Mix and Match Poetry

Ackerman, Diane. "Smell as a Weapon." In *Animal Sense*. Illustrated by Peter Sis. Knopf, 2003.

Bagert, Brod. "Stinky Boys." In *Giant Children*. Illustrated by Tedd Arnold. Dial, 2002.

Bingham, Shirlee Curlee. "Stinky Feet." In *A Bad Case of the Giggles*. Edited by Bruce Lansky. Illustrated by Stephen Carpenter. Meadowbrook, 1994; and *Poetry Party*. Edited by Bruce Lansky. Illustrated by Stephen Carpenter. Meadowbrook, 1996.

Black, Mary Barack. "Dirty Laundry Pile." In *Dirty Laundry Pile: Poems in Different Voices*. Edited by Paul Janeczko. Illustrated by Melissa Sweet. HarperCollins, 2001.

Ciardi, John. "April Fool." In *Knock at a Star.* Rev. ed. Edited by X. J. Kennedy and Dorothy M. Kennedy. Illustrated by Karen Lee Baker. Little, Brown, 1999.

Dodds, Bill. "There Was an Old Woman." In *A Bad Case of the Giggles.* Edited by Bruce Lansky. Illustrated by Stephen Carpenter. Meadowbrook, 1994.

Florian, Douglas. "Fourteen Men Fainted." In *Bing Bang Boing.* Harcourt, 1994.

———. "If You Suffer Smelly Feet." In *Laugh-eteria.* Harcourt, 1999.

Hajdusiewicz, Babs Bell. "Doing Business." In *Kids Pick the Funniest Poems.* Edited by Bruce Lansky. Illustrated by Stephen Carpenter. Meadowbrook, 1991.

Hoberman, Mary Ann. "How Many?" In *Yellow Butter Purple Jelly Red Jam Black Bread.* Illustrated by Chaya Bernstein. Viking, 1981.

Kennedy, X. J. "Skunk Cabbage Stew." In *Exploding Gravy: Poems to Make You Laugh.* Illustrated by Joy Allen. Little, Brown, 2002.

Lansky, Bruce. "I'd Rather," "Ish!" and "My Baby Sister." In *Poetry Party.* Illustrated by Stephen Carpenter. Meadowbrook, 1996.

Prelutsky, Jack. "Deep in Our Refrigerator." In *It's Raining Pigs and Noodles.* Illustrated by James Stevenson. Greenwillow, 2000.

———. "Drumpp the Grump." In *The New Kid on the Block.* Illustrated by James Stevenson. Greenwillow, 1984.

Silverstein, Shel. "Sarah Cynthia Sylvia Stout Would Not Take the Garbage Out." In *Where the Sidewalk Ends.* HarperCollins, 1974.

Stevenson, James. "Garbage Bags." In *Cornflakes.* Greenwillow, 2000.

Tweaking the Program Theme . . .

. . . For Preschoolers

Drop the Coville chapter book selection and the song "Black Socks," and substitute the following picture books:

McCourt, Lisa. *I Love You, Stinky Face.* Illustrated by Cyd Moore. Bridgewater, 1997.

> A mother reassures her child that she would still love her even if the child became a "super smelly skunk." The mother goes on to say that she would

give the child a bath and sprinkle sweet-smelling powder all over her. If she still smelled bad, she would still get hugged. The girl poses the same question in the event she was a big, scary ape; an alligator; a meat-eating dinosaur; a swamp creature; a green alien; and a Cyclops.

Pilkey, Dav. *Big Dog and Little Dog Making a Mistake.* Harcourt, 1999.

Two dogs mistake a skunk for a kitty. They quickly learn that the new creature does not smell like a kitty. Nor do they. "Big Dog smells bad. Little Dog smells bad, too." They head back home and walk in the middle of their owner's tea party. This story can also be found in the following Pilkey collection:

The Complete Adventures of Big Dog and Little Dog. Harcourt, 2003.

. . . For Fifth and Sixth Graders

Drop the Wilson picture book, and replace it with the following oral story:

MacDonald, Margaret Read. "Stinky Spirits." In *Celebrate the World: Twenty Tellable Folktales for Multicultural Festivals.* Wilson, 1994.

Spirits reward a humble boy in this Nigerian folktale. A jealous, greedy boy, however, insults the spirits by complaining about how horrible they stink. His "reward" turns out to be death from horrible diseases that trouble mankind to this day. MacDonald gives the teller a helpful tip about holding one's nose and wrinkling one's face in disgust when sharing the greedy boy's insults.

And Yet Even More Disgusting, Smelly, Stinky Titles for You to Consider

Allen, Jonathan. *Mucky Moose.* Macmillan, 1990.

Brown, Marc. *Arthur's Nose.* Little, Brown, 1976.

Fair, David. *The Fabulous Four Skunks.* Illustrated by Bruce Koscielniak. Houghton Mifflin, 1996.

Gray, Libba Moore. *Is There Room on the Feather Bed?* Illustrated by Nadine Bernard Westcott. Orchard, 1997.

Johnson, Paul Brett. *Bearhide and Crow.* Holiday House, 2000.

Kotzwinkle, William, and Glenn Murray. *Walter, the Farting Dog.* Illustrated by Audrey Colman. Frog, 2001.

———. *Walter, the Farting Dog: Trouble at the Yard Sale.* Illustrated by Audrey Colman. Dutton, 2004.

Levine, Evan. *What's Black and White and Came to Visit?* Illustrated by Betsy Lewin. Orchard, 1994.

Muller, Birte. *Farley Farts.* North-South, 2003.

Munsch, Robert. *Good Families Don't.* Illustrated by Alan Daniel. Dell, 1991.

Sharmat, Marjorie Weinman. *Bartholomew the Bossy.* Macmillan, 1984.

Sonnenschein, Harriet. *Harold's Runaway Nose.* Illustrated by Jurg Obrist. Simon and Schuster, 1989.

SIXTEEN

What's Black and White and Red (Read) All Over?

Lesson Plan at a Glance

POEMS/VIDEO:	*Antarctic Antics* by Judy Sierra
POEM:	"What Is Red?" from *Hailstones and Halibut Bones* by Mary O'Neill
PICTURE BOOK/ART ACTIVITY:	*The Squiggle* by Carole Lexa Schaefer

Preparation and Presentation

This program deals with all things that are either black and white, such as penguins, Dalmatians, zebras, pandas, orca whales, and soccer balls, or are red or shades of red. Be sure your program attire and room decorations reflect these three colors.

OPENING RIDDLES

Start with the popular "What's black and white and red all over?"

Answers include the traditional, "Newspaper," and the slightly more common, "An embarrassed zebra," and finally, the one that elicits a groan from the audience, "A skunk with diaper rash."

Throw in this black-and-white poem-riddle that may very well stump the audience:

> The land was white,
> The sea was black;
> It'll take a good scholar
> To riddle that.
> The answer is: paper and ink.

If the kids can't figure out the answer right away, give them some hints, such as "It's two objects that you use every day" and "What do scholars use a lot of?" (You may have to tell them what a scholar is.)

PICTURE BOOK

Roberts, Lynn. *Rapunzel: A Groovy Fairy Tale*. Illustrated by David Roberts. Abrams, 2003.

This modern-day retelling finds a redheaded Rapunzel trapped in a tall apartment building with a broken elevator. Rapunzel's Aunt Esme, a school lunch lady, keeps Rapunzel trapped in the apartment (complete with David Bowie records and ABBA posters). Rapunzel lets down her red hair to allow

Esme to go in and out of the complex. One day, a musician named Roger calls for Rapunzel to let down her red hair, and that's when the trouble begins.

SHORT STORY SELECTION

King-Smith, Dick. "Little Red Riding Pig." In *Hogsel and Gruntel and Other Animal Stories*. Orchard, 1999.

The title character rides her mountain bike into the forest and encounters a wolf. The beast heads to Granny's house. Granny asks the wolf to come closer and winds up eating him. The twisted ending will surprise the audience.

POEM

O'Neill, Mary. "What Is Black?" In *Hailstones and Halibut Bones*. Rev. ed. Illustrated by John Wallner. Doubleday, 1989.

Read the first in a series of color poems from this modern-day classic.

PICTURE BOOK

Shannon, George. *Lizard's Guest*. Illustrated by Jose Aruego and Ariane Dewey. Greenwillow, 2003.

Lizard steps on Skunk's toes and pays for the accident tenfold. Skunk pretends his injury is worse than it really is and plays on Lizard's guilt. Lizard becomes a slave to Skunk's pampering until he comes up with a clever, yet kindhearted, plan.

POEM

O'Neill, Mary. "What Is White?" In *Hailstones and Halibut Bones*. Rev. ed. Illustrated by John Wallner. Doubleday, 1989.

Read this poem, the second in the series.

ORAL TALE

Hamilton, Martha, and Mitch Weiss. "Do They Play Soccer in Heaven?" In *Stories in My Pocket: Tales Kids Can Tell*. Fulcrum, 1996.

This is a funny, short version of Alvin Schwartz's adaptation of the traditional "The Bad News," found in his collection *More Scary Stories to Tell in the Dark* (HarperCollins, 1984). Instead of a baseball setting, Hamilton and

Weiss tell of two girls, Sue and Kate, who love to play soccer. They grow old together and make a pact. Whoever goes to heaven first must come back and tell the other the title question. Sue later dies. She shows up at Kate's door to say that there's good news and bad news. The good news is that soccer is very popular in heaven. The bad news is that Kate is scheduled to play goalie—tomorrow.

PICTURE BOOK

Fleming, Denise. *Buster.* Holt, 2003.

Meet the most captivating red dog in children's literature since Clifford the Big Red Dog. Buster is upset when a new white cat comes to live with him. He tries to ignore her, but when she has the audacity to change the station on his radio, he runs away and becomes lost.

ORAL TALE

Hamilton, Martha, and Mitch Weiss. "Why the Sun Comes Up When Rooster Crows." In *How and Why Stories: World Tales Kids Can Read and Tell.* August House, 1999.

The People try to call out the hiding sun because the land is freezing. After Tiger and Oriole fail to call up the sun, Rooster is asked to help. Rooster slowly convinces the sun to come up by the third "Cock-a-doodle-doo!" The sun rewards Rooster with a bit of red from the morning sky and places it on rooster's head in the shape of a comb. Rooster struts about to this very day.

POEMS/VIDEO

Sierra, Judy. *Antarctic Antics.* Illustrated by Jose Aruego and Ariane Dewey. Harcourt, 1998.

This collection of humorous penguin poems has been captured in an excellent public-performance-rights eighteen-minute video by Weston Woods (2000). Read a few of the poems, show select clips from the video, or let the audience listen to the recorded versions on cassette or CD (also distributed by Weston Woods). The video won the Andrew Carnegie Medal for Excellence in Children's Video. It was also named an ALA Notable Video and was chosen one of *Booklist's* Top 10 Poetry Videos. There are amusing musical parodies of the Beach Boys, Bob Dylan, and "We Are the World." Favorite poems include "Regurgitate," describing how baby penguins are fed; "I Am

Looking for My Mother," which relates how infant penguins recognize their mothers by sound; "Belly Sliding," a look at penguin playtime; and "Predator Riddles," which carries the riddle format started at the beginning of the program. This is definitely one of the better children's videos based on a children's book and one of the few videos I use in live story programs.

POEM

O'Neill, Mary. "What Is Red?" In *Hailstones and Halibut Bones*. Rev. ed. Illustrated by John Wallner. Doubleday, 1989; and in *The Random House Book of Poetry for Children*. Edited by Jack Prelutsky. Illustrated by Arnold Lobel. Random House, 1983.

Lead the upcoming red-themed picture book and art activity by having the kids think about all things red. This poem includes a sunset, braveness, sunburn, and more.

PICTURE BOOK/ART ACTIVITY

Schaefer, Carole Lexa. *The Squiggle*. Illustrated by Pierr Morgan. Crown, 1996.

Normally, I wouldn't use this younger picture book with the school-age crowd, but it lends itself to the follow-up art activity so well. A little girl sees a red squiggly line on the sidewalk. In her imagination, it becomes part of a dragon, the Great Wall of China, an acrobat's tightrope, and more. After reading the book, give the audience members pieces of different-colored strands of yarn. Ask them to shift the yarn into different shapes. Once they have a shape, they can draw a background scene to reveal what their shape is a part of. Glue the yarn to the paper and hang the finished works in the library or school.

Finish the program by providing red treats, such as apples, strawberries, red candies, red licorice, and perhaps some Good & Plenty candy for a "black-and-white-and-pink" touch.

Mix and Match Picture Books

Book, Rita. *My Soccer Mom from Mars*. Illustrated by Amy Wummer. Grosset and Dunlop, 2001.

Ryan's soccer teams calls themselves the Half and Half's because half the team is made up of boys and the other half is made up of girls. They all wear black-and-white uniforms like dairy cows. Ryan is embarrassed of his mother.

She sends him notes such as "Roses are red / Soccer balls are black and white / I love you a lot." She jumps up and down on the sideline clanging a cowbell and clad in black and white. "She looked like a big soccer ball with legs." Share the clever wordplay on the author's name. Rita Book is a pseudonym for authors Joan Holub and E. A. Hass.

Bunting, Eve. *Whales Passing.* Illustrated by Lambert Davis. Scholastic, 2003.

A boy and his father observe and comment on a pod of black-and-white orca whales. The boy wonders if the whales are observing and commenting on the two humans onshore.

Kellogg, Steven. *A Penguin Pup for Pinkerton.* Dial, 2001.

Pinkerton, the black-and-white Great Dane, learns that father emperor penguins cradle their eggs on their feet. Pinkerton commandeers a black-and-white football and cradles it on his feet, waiting for it to hatch. Billy, the upset owner of the football, sets out to prove that "as a penguin parent, Pinkerton is a flop!"

London, Jonathan. *Froggy Plays Soccer.* Illustrated by Frank Remkiewicz. Viking, 1999.

Froggy suits up for the big soccer game with a "zap, zeep, zoop." During the game, he touches the black-and-white soccer ball with his hands, causing his green face to turn red from embarrassment. He finally sticks his hands in his armpits, his pockets, and his mouth before kicking the game-winning goal. In the end, the audience learns the only time to use your hands in soccer is to high-five your teammates. Ask the audience to high-five each other for being good listeners.

Shields, Carol Diggory. *Martian Rock.* Illustrated by Scott Nash. Candlewick, 1999.

Aliens search our solar system to learn "if life could exist somewhere else in the stars." They check out each planet without luck. Before heading home (they were "fresh out of socks and clean underwear"), they try Earth. The only earthlings they encounter are penguins. The aliens join the earthlings in Follow-the-Leader, Slippery Sliding, Tummy-Toboggan, and Find-Me-I'm-Hiding before returning home.

Sturges, Philemon. *The Little Red Hen (Makes a Pizza).* Illustrated by Amy Walrod. Dutton, 1999.

The Little Red Hen makes pizza, not bread, in this retelling of the classic story. She asks if anyone has a pizza pan. A duck, a dog, and a cat reply "Not

I." The Little Red Hen goes through the whole process of buying ingredients and making the pizza, all the while asking for help and getting a chorus of "Not I's." In the end, the three other animals help the Little Red Hen eat the pizza. When she asks who will wash the dishes, the three dive right in.

Wahl, Jan. *Three Pandas*. Illustrated by Naava. Boyds Mills, 2000.

Yip, Yap, and Yep go out to see the world. They find jobs and shelter in the city. They play bamboo flutes on the street corners. They eventually head back home. There is a brief story within the story that explains why pandas are black and white.

Wood, Audrey. *The Red Racer*. Simon and Schuster, 1996.

Nona dreams of owning a new Deluxe Red Racer bicycle to replace her "ugly bike." She has one wicked thought after another to dispose of it. Friendly neighbors keep rescuing the old bike, much to her dismay. Her parents finally jazz up her old bike to create a new-looking, red "most beautiful bicycle in the whole world."

Mix and Match Chapter Book Selections

Atwater, Richard, and Florence Atwater. *Mr. Popper's Penguins*. Little, Brown, 1938.

A housepainter is surprised when a crate arrives at his house containing a live penguin. Read chapter 6, "More Trouble." A policeman arrives at their house in response to a complaint about the penguin. "What is it—a giant parrot?"

Cleary, Beverly. *Henry Huggins*. Morrow, 1950.

Henry enters his dog, Ribsy, in a dog show in the chapter "The Pale Pink Dog." Start with the sentence, "Henry had an idea," and read to the end of the chapter. Henry pours talcum powder on Ribsy to whiten him up. To Henry's horror, the powder is pink and so is Ribsy. After Ribsy gets into a fight with another dog, he is awarded "the most unusual dog in the show."

Nixon, Joan Lowery. *Gus and Gertie and the Lucky Charms*. SeaStar, 2001.

Two penguins travel to the Animals' Winter Olympics to participate in synchronized swimming (they appear wearing matching swimming caps). Read chapter 2. The two find themselves in a crowded registration tent, and the official informs them that there are no swimming events in the Winter

Olympics. The chapter ends with the line, "Gus didn't have a chance to answer because at that moment someone screamed."

Smith, Dodie. *The Hundred and One Dalmatians*. Viking, 1956.

Many kids are familiar with the Disney movie based on Smith's modern-day classic. Dalmatian puppies are kidnapped by the evil Cruella De Vil. Read the second half of chapter 1, "The Happy Couple." We meet Cruella. Begin with the sentence, "At that moment the peace was shattered by an extremely strident motor horn," and read to the end of the chapter. Cruella makes it clear that black-and-white Dalmatian fur would go well with her black-and-white car and black-and-white hair. Read a few more lines into chapter 2, "The Puppies Arrive." Everything at Cruella's dinner party tastes like pepper, and Mr. Darling figures out that De Vil stands for *devil*.

Mix and Match Oral Tales

Hoffman, Mary. *The Barefoot Book of Brother and Sister Tales*. Illustrated by Emma Shaw-Smith. Barefoot Books, 2000.

A mean stepmother is jealous of her husband, son, and daughter in this parallel Cinderella story. She arranges to have the kindly Red Cow killed. The spirit of the Red Cow watches over the children and helps them achieve lives of wealth and comfort.

Van Laan, Nancy. "Why Fox Is Red." In *In a Circle Long Ago: A Treasury of Native Lore from North America*. Illustrated by Lisa Desimini. Knopf, 1995.

A fox gets so angry at his inability to get to the geese swimming in the lake that he howls and turns red from anger. Only the tip of his tail is unmarked.

Mix and Match Craft Activity

Ross, Kathy. *Crafts for Kids Who Are Wild about Polar Life*. Illustrated by Sharon Lane Holm. Millbrook, 1998.

This resource includes instructions for creating a "Penguin Pin," made out of wooden ice-cream spoons; a "Rockhopper Penguin," made with black and orange construction paper and a plastic sandwich bag filled with white Styrofoam packing pieces; a black-and-white "Hands and Foot Arctic Tern"; and more.

Mix and Match Poetry

Cedering, Siv. "The Red Gloves." In *Dirty Laundry Pile: Poems in Different Voices*. Edited by Paul B. Janeczko. Illustrated by Melissa Sweet. HarperCollins, 2001.

Chaikin, Miriam. "A Cardinal in the Yard." In *Don't Step on the Sky: A Handful of Haiku*. Illustrated by Hiroe Nakata. Holt, 2002.

Esbensen, Barbara Juster. "Cardinal." In *Beauty of the Beast: Poems from the Animal Kingdom*. Edited by Jack Prelutsky. Illustrated by Meilo So. Knopf, 1997.

Florian, Douglas. "Mrs. Mason's Long Red Hair." In *Bing Bang Boing*. Harcourt, 1994.

Hallock, Grace Tabor. "Red-Winged Blackbird." In *The Twentieth Century Children's Poetry Treasury*. Edited by Jack Prelutsky. Illustrated by Meilo So. Knopf, 1999.

Hoberman, Mary Ann. "How Many," "Panda," "Penguin," and "Tapir." In *The Llama Who Had No Pajama*. Illustrated by Betty Fraser. Harcourt, 1998.

Hughes, Ted. "Skunk." In *Beauty of the Beast: Poems from the Animal Kingdom*. Edited by Jack Prelutsky. Illustrated by Meilo So. Knopf, 1997; and in *A Zooful of Animals*. Edited by William Cole. Illustrated by Lynn Munsinger. Houghton Mifflin, 1992.

Kennedy, X. J. "Skunk and Stink." In *Exploding Gravy: Poems to Make You Laugh*. Illustrated by Joy Allen. Little, Brown, 2002.

Kuskin, Karla. "Summer Is Gone." In *Moon, Have You Met My Mother?* Illustrated by Sergio Ruzzier. Laura Geringer, 2003.

Lewis, J. Patrick. "Red Radish, Green Garnish." In *The Bookworm's Feast: A Potluck of Poems*. Illustrated by John O'Brien. Dial, 1999.

Numeroff, Laura. "My Friend's Freckles" and "Spots." In *Sometimes I Wonder If Poodles Like Noodles*. Illustrated by Tim Bowers. Simon and Schuster, 1999.

Prelutsky, Jack. "The Frogs Wore Red Suspenders" and "Red Horse, White Horse, Black Horse, Grey." In *The Frogs Wore Red Suspenders*. Illustrated by Petra Mathers. Greenwillow, 2002.

———. "I Have a Pet Tomato." In *It's Raining Pigs and Noodles*. Illustrated by James Stevenson. Greenwillow, 2000.

———. "Its Fangs Were Red." In *The New Kid on the Block*. Illustrated by James Stevenson. Greenwillow, 1984.

————. "Penguins," "An Unsavory Tomato," and "When Daddy Sat on a Tomato." In *A Pizza the Size of the Sun.* Illustrated by James Stevenson. Greenwillow, 1996.

————. "Unhappy South Pole Penguin." In *Something Big Has Been Here.* Illustrated by James Stevenson. Greenwillow, 1990.

Silverstein, Shel. "Red Flowers for You." In *Falling Up.* HarperCollins, 1996.

————. "Zebra Question." In *A Light in the Attic.* HarperCollins, 1981.

Spilka, Arnold. "Slippery Sam." In *Read-Aloud Rhymes for the Very Young.* Edited by Jack Prelutsky. Illustrated by Marc Brown. Knopf, 1986.

Stevenson, James. "Point of View" and "The Red Ball." In *Corn-Fed.* Greenwillow, 2002.

Unobagha, Uzo. "Raced the Striped Zebra across the Plains." In *Off to the Sweet Shores of Africa and Other Talking Drum Rhymes.* Illustrated by Julia Cairns. Chronicle, 2000.

Tweaking the Program Theme . . .

. . . *For Preschoolers*

Drop the King-Smith chapter book selection and the Roberts picture book, and substitute the following picture books:

Murphy, Mary. *Please Be Quiet!* Houghton Mifflin, 1999.

> A young penguin makes a lot of noise. The audience can, of course, help make the same noises. The penguin parent yells, "Please, be quiet!" and "Outside, please!" After playing with other animal friends, the penguin cleverly plays indoors with socks on its feet: "Hush, hush, hush."

Walton, Rick. *That's My Dog!* Illustrated by Julia Gorton. Putnam, 2001.

> This fun cumulative story adds adjective after adjective describing the dog. Not only is this dog a red dog, he's a "big red happy muddy smart bouncy slobbery sneaky stinky dog!"

. . . *For Fifth and Sixth Graders*

Drop the Fleming and Shannon picture books, and substitute the following selections:

Garner, James Finn. "Little Red Riding Hood." In *Politically Correct Bedtime Stories*. Macmillan, 1994.

> Red brings Grandma a basket full of "fat-free, sodium-free snacks." When the "passing woodchopper person (or log-fuel technician, as he preferred to be called)" bursts in to save the day, Red Riding Hood, Grandma, and the wolf call him "sexist" and "speciesist."

Gutman, Dan. *The Million Dollar Kick*. Hyperion, 2001.

> Whisper is a misfit at school and in sports. She mentally replays the time she kicked a goal in her own team's net. Her sister enters Whisper in a contest to kick a soccer ball past a professional women's soccer goalie for $1 million. Read the second half of chapter 4, "A Million Dollars Is a Million Dollars." Start with the sentence, "'So,' Dad said as we sat down to dinner that night, 'what did you all do today?'" and read until the end of the chapter.

And Yet Even More Black-and-White- and Red-Themed Books for You to Consider

Artell, Mike. *Petite Rouge: A Cajun Red Riding Hood*. Illustrated by Jim Harris. Dial, 2001.

Butterfield, Moira. *Who Am I? I Am Black and White*. Thameside, 2002.

Christelow, Eileen. *Henry and the Red Stripes*. Clarion, 1982.

French, Vivian. *Red Hen and Sly Fox*. Illustrated by Sally Hobson. Simon and Schuster, 1994.

Gantos, Jack. *Rotten Ralph*. Illustrated by Nicole Rubel. Houghton Mifflin, 1976.

Gay, Michel. *Zee*. Clarion, 2003.

Johnson, Paul Brett. *The Pig Who Ran a Red Light*. Orchard, 1999.

Levine, Evan. *What's Black and White and Came to Visit?* Illustrated by Betsy Lewin. Orchard, 1994.

McKee, David. *Zebra's Hiccups*. Simon and Schuster, 1993.

Monsell, Mary Elise. *The Mysterious Cases of Mr. Pin*. Atheneum, 1989.

Munsch, Robert. *The Fire Station*. Illustrated by Michael Martchenko. Annick, 1991.

Mwenye Hadithi. *Greedy Zebra*. Illustrated by Adrienne Kennaway. Little, Brown, 1984.

Patrick, Denise Lewis. *Red Dancing Shoes.* Illustrated by James Ransome. Tambourine, 1993.

Perlman, Janet. *Cinderella Penguin; or, The Little Glass Flipper.* Viking, 1992.

Wood, Audrey, and Don Wood. *The Little Mouse, the Red, Ripe Strawberry, and the Big, Hungry Bear.* Illustrated by Don Wood. Child's Play, 1984.

Zion, Gene. *Harry, the Dirty Dog.* Illustrated by Margaret Bloy Graham. Harper, 1956.

SEVENTEEN

Underwear and
Other Unruly Clothing

Lesson Plan at a Glance

PICTURE BOOK: *Underwear Do's and Don'ts* by
Todd Parr

SONG: "God Bless My Underwear" from the
recording *See You Later, Alligator* by
Hans Mayer

PICTURE BOOK: *The Skeleton in the Closet* by Alice Schertle

POEM: "The Reason Skeletons Don't Wear
Clothes" from *Two Skeletons on the
Telephone and Other Poems from Tough
City* by Paul Duggan

PICTURE BOOK/READER'S THEATER: *The Kettles Get New Clothes* by
Dayle Ann Dodds

POEM: "Hand-Me Downs" by Bob Zanger from *A
Bad Case of the Giggles*, edited by
Bruce Lansky

PICTURE BOOK: *Grandpa's Overalls* by Tony Crunk

POEM: "I Hate My Hat" from *You Read to Me, I'll
Read to You* by Mary Ann Hoberman

CHAPTER BOOK SELECTION:	*Captain Underpants and the Big, Bad Battle of the Bionic Booger Boy, Part 1: The Night of the Nasty Nostril Nuggets* by Dav Pilkey
ACTIVITY:	Captain Underpants Games

Preparation and Presentation

Is there a more charged word for kids than *underwear?* Use it frequently when advertising this program. If you are brave enough, don a pair of wild boxer shorts over your slacks or jeans. (I prefer boxers with smiley faces, while others prefer hearts.)

PICTURE BOOK

Parr, Todd. *Underwear Do's and Don'ts.* Little, Brown, 2000.

Don't let the toddler book format fool you. I know one middle school teacher who uses this book with great success. The humor is ideal for the school-age crowd. Here are some examples: "Do put your clean underwear away. Don't put it in the freezer"; "Do wear new underwear on the first day of school. Don't bring it for show-and-tell"; and "Do go shopping for underwear with a hippo. Don't let her try it on."

SONG

Mayer, Hans. "God Bless My Underwear." In *See You Later, Alligator* (recording). Windwall Records, 1997.

A kids' choir joins Mayer in this short ditty to the tune of "God Bless America." "From the washer to the dryer to my backpack to my rear . . ." You can order the recording at www.hansmayer.com.

PICTURE BOOK

Schertle, Alice. *The Skeleton in the Closet.* Illustrated by Curtis Jobling. HarperCollins, 2003.

A skeleton slowly creaks up a boy's stairs in this humorous story. The skeleton demands clothing and rummages through the boy's underwear shelf, puts on "spaceman underpants," and more. The final images of the skeleton are hilarious. He is donned in a rainbow stocking cap, a red-and-white-striped scarf, jacket, blue jeans, and "bedroom slipper bears."

POEM

Duggan, Paul. "The Reason Skeletons Don't Wear Clothes." In *Two Skeletons on the Telephone and Other Poems from Tough City*. Illustrated by Daniel Sylvestre. Millbrook, 1999.

Skeletons walk around "in the buff" for many reasons, including the fact that their underwear "just sags and slumps." This is a perfect companion to the Schertle picture book.

PICTURE BOOK/READER'S THEATER

Dodds, Dayle Ann. *The Kettles Get New Clothes*. Illustrated by Jill McElmurry. Candlewick, 2002.

The Kettle family drives into town to buy plain and simple clothes. However, Monsieur Pip dresses them in paisley, stripes, checks, and dots. This is an ideal book to adapt to a reader's theater script as each family member vocalizes what's wrong with Monsieur Pip's recommendations. Assign one narrator and readers for Father Kettle, Mother Kettle, Sister Kettle, Brother Kettle, and Baby Kettle (who only smiles and cries). Add a line at the end to let the audience know that Baby Kettle happily emerges from the dressing room clad in paisley, stripes, checks, and dots.

POEM

Zanger, Bob. "Hand-Me Downs." In *A Bad Case of the Giggles*. Edited by Bruce Lansky. Illustrated by Stephen Carpenter. Meadowbrook, 1994.

A boy complains about getting dresses, high heels, and similar apparel as hand-me-downs from his older sisters.

PICTURE BOOK

Crunk, Tony. *Grandpa's Overalls*. Illustrated by Scott Nash. Orchard, 2001.

Grandpa's overalls run away, and Grandpa is upset because he can't do his farm chores wearing nothing but his "long-handled drawers." This leads to a big chase scene until the overalls disappear. In the end, the overalls reappear dancing with Grandma's nightgown.

POEM

Hoberman, Mary Ann. "I Hate My Hat." In *You Read to Me, I'll Read to You.* Illustrated by Michael Emberley. Little, Brown, 2001.

Ask for a volunteer from the audience to join you in this poem designed for two voices. A raccoon can't decide what type of hat to wear. The second raccoon is seen wearing a fez in the book.

CHAPTER BOOK SELECTION

Pilkey, Dav. *Captain Underpants and the Big, Bad Battle of the Bionic Booger Boy, Part 1: The Night of the Nasty Nostril Nuggets.* Scholastic, 2003.

What's a program about underwear without Pilkey's overwhelmingly popular Captain Underpants? Read chapters 1 to 5 of this volume. George and Harold switch a school sign that reads "Please Wash Your Hands after Using the Toilet" to "Please Wash Your Hands in the Toilet" (which we see student Melvin Sneedly doing). For their demonstration speech, the two boys show how to make a "Squishy" (it involves a toilet-seat lid slammed down on two packets of ketchup). Melvin's demonstration speech is his invention, the Combine-O-Tron 2000, which creates a cyborg hamster. Finish the short chapters with the two-panel cartoon of the hamster spanking Melvin with a paddle.

ACTIVITY

Captain Underpants Games

End the program with a few games found on Pilkey's web site, www.pilkey .com/index.php, or visit the PUBlic Libraries, Young Adults, and Children (PUBYAC) online discussion group, made up of librarians, many of whom have hosted Captain Underpants parties and shared their successes. Be sure to throw in a few of the groaner jokes found at this site. Example: "What does lightning wear beneath its clothes? Thunderwear." Visit the PUBYAC Archives at www.pallasinc.com/pubyac/Archives.htm.

A few of the more successful games held in my local libraries have been "The Underwear Fling," which involves stretching the elastic of a brand-new pair of boy's briefs and see who can fling it the farthest; and "The Toilet Paper Roll Toss," in which rolls of unopened toilet paper are tossed into a bucket made to simulate a toilet. One library was able to convince the local plumbing supply store to loan a brand-new toilet seat for this game. It sat in the middle of the children's room for an entire day!

Mix and Match Picture Books

Brown, Marc. *Arthur's Underwear.* Little, Brown, 1999.

After Binky rips his pants in class and everyone laughs, Arthur starts dreaming that he himself starts showing up everywhere in his underwear. His classmates learn about his new fears and, much to his dismay, find this hilarious.

Gerstein, Mordicai. *Stop Those Pants!* Harcourt, 1998.

Murray tries everything to get his pants on. He even enlists the help of his socks, his T-shirt, and his belt. Murray's clothes talk to him, even his underwear.

Hoberman, Mary Ann. *Bill Grogan's Goat.* Illustrated by Nadine Bernard Westcott. Little, Brown, 2002.

The traditional song includes the lyrics, "Bill Grogan's goat / Was feeling fine / Ate three red shirts / Right off the line / That goat he bucked / With might and main / Coughed up those shirts / And flagged the train." Hoberman expands the story line by having the train engineer invite the goat on board. The goat shares the shirts with other animals on the train.

Munsch, Robert. *We Share Everything!* Illustrated by Michael Martchenko. Scholastic, 1999.

Two kindergartners don't understand the concept of sharing. They scream and yell when things don't go their way. Let the audience scream and yell with them. The kids' extremely upbeat teacher tries her best to teach them how to share. "We share everything," she says. The two kids take sharing to the extreme, first by swapping their shoes, then their shirts, and then their pants.

Uegaki, Chieri. *Suki's Kimono.* Illustrated by Stephane Jorisch. Kids Can, 2003.

Suki wears a kimono her first day of first grade, much to the embarrassment of her two contemporary-clad sisters. Some of Suki's new classmates make fun of her, but after she shares her wooden clogs and a dance, the whole class applauds.

Whatley, Bruce, and Rosie Smith. *Captain Pajamas.* Illustrated by Bruce Whatley. HarperCollins, 2000.

This story of Brian, who tries to save his family from aliens with the help of "his trusty dog, Shadow," is presented in a large-framed, comic book style. The aliens turn out to be a toy, Shadow in the bathtub, Shadow in the refrigerator, and Shadow (again) with the TV remote. Read Brian's lines as a larger-than-life superhero: "I, Captain Pajamas, Defender of the Universe, have come to save you!"

Mix and Match Chapter Book Selections

Cleary, Beverly. *Ramona and Her Mother.* Morrow, 1979.

Ramona likes her new pajamas so much that she wears them under her school clothes. She becomes so warm in class that her teacher is worried that Ramona is getting sick. Ramona eventually confesses that she's hot because of her pajamas. She can't take them off because she's not wearing any underpants. Her teacher assures her that it's okay to go without underwear for one day: "Underwear—pooh!"

Lawrence, Michael. *The Killer Underpants.* Dutton, 2000.

An old woman curses Jiggy. She tells him, "Beware the very next thing you touch." That happens to be a new pair of "one hundred percent cotton jersey multicolored" underpants. Later, when Jiggy tries to remove them, they refuse to budge. Read chapter 8. Jiggy's gym teacher gets mad when Jiggy wears the underwear in the boys' shower.

Mix and Match Songs

Polisar, Barry Louis. "Underwear." In *Teacher's Favorites* (recording). Rainbow Morning Music, 1993.

Play the recording, and the audience will join in the catchy chorus to this ode to underwear: "Underwear is everywhere, but mostly underneath . . ."

Scruggs, Joe. "Big Underwear." In *Ants* (recording). Shadow Play Records, 1994.

This ode to overly large underwear would provide a great soundtrack for a choreographed show.

Mix and Match Poetry

Brown, Calef. "Dutch Sneakers." In *Dutch Sneakers and Flea Keepers.* Houghton Mifflin, 2000.

Cole, William. "The Panteater." In *The Place My Words Are Looking For.* Edited by Paul B. Janeczko. Bradbury, 1990.

Dodds, Bill. "Could Have Been Worse." In *Kids Pick the Funniest Poems.* Edited by Bruce Lansky. Illustrated by Stephen Carpenter. Meadowbrook, 1991.

Hoberman, Mary Ann. "The Llama Who Had No Pajama." In *The Llama Who Had No Pajama.* Illustrated by Betty Fraser. Harcourt, 1998; and in *Yellow Butter Purple Jelly Red Jam Black Bread.* Illustrated by Chaya Bernstein. Viking, 1981.

Knaus, Linda. "A Very Stubborn Polar Bear." In *A Bad Case of the Giggles.* Edited by Bruce Lansky. Illustrated by Stephen Carpenter. Meadowbrook, 1994.

Kredenser, Gail. "Polar Bear." In *Read-Aloud Rhymes for the Very Young.* Edited by Jack Prelutsky. Illustrated by Marc Brown. Knopf, 1986.

Kuskin, Karla. "A Boy Had a Mother Who Bought Him a Hat." In *Moon, Have You Met My Mother?* Illustrated by Sergio Ruzzier. Laura Geringer, 2003.

————. "Winter Clothes." In *The Random House Book of Poetry for Children.* Edited by Jack Prelutsky. Illustrated by Arnold Lobel. Random House, 1983.

Prelutsky, Jack. "As Soon as Fred Gets Out of Bed." In *Something Big Has Been Here.* Illustrated by James Stevenson. Greenwillow, 1990.

————. "I Wear the Most Amazing Shoes" and "I'm Wearing an Enchanted Hat." In *A Pizza the Size of the Sun.* Illustrated by James Stevenson. Greenwillow, 1996.

————. "Ma, Don't Throw That Shirt Out." In *The New Kid on the Block.* Illustrated by James Stevenson. Greenwillow, 1984.

Soto, Gary. "Left Shoe on the Right Foot." In *Canto Familiar.* Illustrated by Annika Nelson. Harcourt, 1995.

Viorst, Judith. "Sad Underwear." In *Sad Underwear and Other Complications.* Illustrated by Richard Hull. Atheneum, 1995.

Tweaking the Program Theme . . .

. . . For Preschoolers

Drop the reader's theater option of Dodds's picture book and Pilkey's Captain Underpants selection and activities, and read the following picture book:

Dolan, Penny. *Mary and the Fairy.* Illustrated by Deborah Allwright. Picture Window Books, 2003.

> Mary has nothing to wear to the party. She goes through several emotions as a fairy guesses which color gown to grant. "The green made Mary's tummy feel wobbly." In the end, Mary wears a spacesuit, for the party turns out to be a costume party.

. . . For Fifth and Sixth Graders

Drop the Crunk and Schertle picture books, and substitute the following short story:

Crutcher, Chris. "A Brief Moment in the Life of Angus Bethune." In *Athletic Shorts: Six Short Stories.* Greenwillow, 1991.

> Angus is an overweight student. He's nervous about taking the popular Melissa to the Winter Ball. His rental tuxedo is purple, and he's afraid that he looks like a giant plum. Begin with the sentence, "My dad was in an hour ago, looking sadly at me sitting here on the side of my bed in my underwear," and read to "'The tux looks fine, Angus.' He left."

And Yet a Few More Embarrassing Books about Underwear and Unruly Clothing for You to Consider

Anholt, Laurence. *The Emperor's Underwear.* Illustrated by Arthur Robins. Meadowbrook, 1999.

Barrett, Judi. *Animals Should Definitely Not Wear Clothing.* Illustrated by Ron Barrett. Atheneum, 1970.

Calmenson, Stephanie. *The Principal's New Clothes.* Illustrated by Denise Brunkus. Scholastic, 1989.

Cooke, Kaz. *The Terrible Underpants.* Hyperion, 2003.

Coville, Bruce. *There's an Alien in My Underwear.* Pocket, 2001.

Griffiths, Andy. *The Day My Butt Went Psycho.* Scholastic, 2003.

Lasky, Kathryn. *The Emperor's Old Clothes.* Illustrated by David Catrow. Harcourt, 1999.

Lattimore, Deborah Nourse. *I Wonder What's Under There? A Brief History of Underwear.* Illustrated by David A. Carter. Browndeer, 1998.

Little, Mimi Otey. *Daddy Has a Pair of Striped Shorts*. Farrar, Straus and Giroux, 1990.

Lloyd, Sam. *What Color Is Your Underwear?* Cartwheel, 2004.

London, Jonathan. *Froggy Gets Dressed*. Illustrated by Frank Remkiewicz. Viking, 1992.

Miles, Betty. *The Secret Life of the Underwear Champ*. Knopf, 1981.

Monsell, Mary Elise. *Underwear!* Illustrated by Lynn Munsinger. Whitman, 1988.

Munsch, Robert. *Thomas' Snowsuit*. Illustrated by Michael Martchenko. Annick, 1985.

Spinelli, Jerry. *Who Ran My Underwear Up the Flagpole?* Scholastic, 1992.

EIGHTEEN

Catching Some *Zzzzz*'s

Lesson Plan at a Glance

SONG:	"Zag Zig" from the recording *Zag Zig* by Tom Chapin
PICTURE BOOK:	*Beautiful Blackbird* by Ashley Bryan
PICTURE BOOK:	*Mount Olympus Basketball* by Kevin O'Malley
SHORT STORY SELECTION:	"Zlateh the Goat" from *Zlateh the Goat and Other Stories* by Isaac Bashevis Singer
PICTURE BOOK:	"The Zax" from *The Sneetches and Other Stories* by Dr. Seuss
POEM:	"Zebra Question" from *A Light in the Attic* by Shel Silverstein
PICTURE BOOK/CREATIVE DRAMATICS:	*The Z Was Zapped: A Play in Twenty-Six Acts* by Chris Van Allsburg
PICTURE BOOK:	*A Lion Named Shirley Williamson* by Bernard Waber
ACTIVITY:	How the Z was "Zapped" in Other Alphabet Books
CRAFT ACTIVITY:	Making Zoo Flakes Based on the Book *Zoo Flakes ABC* by Will C. Howell

Preparation and Presentation

This program features the letter Z, whether the title of the book starts with Z, a character's name starts with Z, the story is from a country that starts with Z, or someone in the story is catching some Zs (snoring). This theme is a good counterpoint to the "A-1" theme in chapter 1.

SONG

Chapin, Tom. "Zag Zig." In *Zag Zig* (recording). Sony Wonder, 1994.

Play this recording as the audience enters the story program area. Chapin sings about a raindrop that goes "flop flip" instead of "flip flop," a church bell that goes "dong ding" instead of "ding dong," a donkey who goes "haw hee" instead of "hee haw," and the kids who go "zag zig" because everyone else goes "zig zag." This song is also available on the following Chapin recording:

> *Great Big Fun for the Very Little One* (recording). Music for Little People, 2001.

PICTURE BOOK

Bryan, Ashley. *Beautiful Blackbird.* Atheneum, 2003.

This beautiful picture book is based on a story from Zambia, and thus a good choice for our Z theme. The colorful birds of Africa claim Blackbird as the most beautiful bird of all. "Black is beautiful." Blackbird, in turn, paints black markings on each of the other birds, reminding them that "color on the outside is not what's on the inside."

PICTURE BOOK

O'Malley, Kevin. *Mount Olympus Basketball.* Walker, 2003.

This hilarious picture book features the Greek gods, led by team captain Zeus, playing basketball against the Mortals, who include Hercules, Achilles, and Jason. Grab a partner to help you read this text, which is written as sports announcers delivering a play-by-play account of the battle. In the end, when the Mortals come close, Zeus gets mad and scores basket after basket. The final score is "Gods: 2,678,352, Mortals: 6."

SHORT STORY SELECTION

Singer, Isaac Bashevis. "Zlateh the Goat." In *Zlateh the Goat and Other Stories.* Illustrated by Maurice Sendak. Harper, 1966.

This quiet but powerful story tells of young Aaron, who has to sell his beloved goat, Zlateh. On the way to town, the two get caught in a heavy snowstorm. They find shelter in a haystack and keep each other company for three days. Zlateh eats the hay and in turn gives Aaron milk and keeps him warm. You may want to cut a few lines to make the selection shorter, but Singer's masterful writing will still captivate the audience. The story can also be found in the following Singer collection:

Stories for Children. Farrar, Straus and Giroux, 1984.

PICTURE BOOK

Dr. Seuss. "The Zax." In *The Sneetches and Other Stories.* Random House, 1961.

The North-Going Zax bumps into the South-Going Zax and both are too stubborn to move out of the way. There they remain to this very day, "unbudged in their tracks."

POEM

Silverstein, Shel. "Zebra Question." In *A Light in the Attic.* HarperCollins, 1981.

A boy asks a zebra that age-old question, "Are you black with white stripes or white with black stripes?" The zebra in turn asks several questions of the boy to which the boy replies, "I'll never ask a zebra / About stripes / Again."

PICTURE BOOK/CREATIVE DRAMATICS

Van Allsburg, Chris. *The Z Was Zapped: A Play in Twenty-Six Acts.* Houghton Mifflin, 1987.

Take a cue from the subtitle and have the kids stand up and act out how they perceive the action "on the stage." For example, during the line, "The J was rather Jittery," the kids could shake like they have the jitters. For the line, "The M was beginning to Melt," the kids could slowly "melt" to the floor. Some of the letters are challenging, such as "The E was slowly Evaporating" and "The U was abruptly Uprooted." There are no right or wrong actions. Let the kids make any type of movement that vaguely resembles how the letters are acting and be prepared to lead by example.

PICTURE BOOK

Waber, Bernard. *A Lion Named Shirley Williamson.* Houghton Mifflin, 1996.

Now that the kids have shaken their sillies out, they'll be ready for a slightly longer story. Waber's picture book is one of the funniest picture books on the market for the elementary-age crowd. I can't even keep a straight face saying the title. Shirley Williamson is the hit of the zoo (our *Z* connection). We learn how she got her name, why the other lions are jealous of her, and what happens when the zoo's board of directors try to change her name to Bongo.

ACTIVITY

How the *Z* Was "Zapped" in Other Alphabet Books

There are many creative alphabet books on the market that are better suited for the school-age crowd than for preschoolers. Set several titles out for display, and have the kids examine how each illustrator portrays the letter *Z*. You might want to start out by showing the audience the following imaginative alphabet book:

Agee, Jon. *Z Goes Home.* Hyperion, 2003.

Here is a list of other imaginative alphabet books to share with this age group, with a note about how the letter *Z* is portrayed in each book.

Allen, Susan, and Jane Lindaman. *Read Anything Good Lately?* Illustrated by Vicky Enright. Millbrook, 2003. (The zodiac at the zoo.)

Aylesworth, Jim. *Naughty Little Monkeys.* Illustrated by Henry Cole. Dutton, 2003. (The naughty little monkeys go back to the zoo.)

Bowen, Betsy. *Antler, Bear, Canoe: A Northwoods Alphabet Year.* Little, Brown, 1991. (Zero.)

Boynton, Sandra. *A Is for Angry: An Animal and Adjective Alphabet.* Workman, 1983. (Zany and zzzzzzzz . . .)

Capucilli, Alyssa Satin. *Mrs. McTats and Her Houseful of Cats.* Illustrated by Joan Rankin. Margaret K. McElderry, 2001. (Twenty-six cats and a dog named Zoom.)

Cline-Ransom, Lesa. *Quilt Alphabet.* Illustrated by James Ransome. Holiday House, 2001. (Zigzag.)

Crosbie, Michael J. *Arches to Zigzags: An Architecture ABC.* Illustrated by Steve Rosenthal and Kit Rosenthal. Abrams, 2000. (Zigzag.)

Demarest, Chris. *The Cowboy ABC.* DK, 1999. (The sound at the end of the day.)

DeVicq de Cumptich, Roberto. *Bembo's Zoo: An Animal ABC Book.* Holt, 2000. (Zebra.)

Edwards, Wallace. *Alphabeasts*. Kids Can, 2002. (Zebra.)

Ehlert, Lois. *Eating the Alphabet: Fruits and Vegetables from A to Z*. Harcourt, 1989. (Zucchini.)

Hopkins, Lee Bennett. *Alphathought: Alphabet Poems*. Illustrated by Marla Baggetta. Boyds Mills, 2003. (Zoos.)

Johnson, Stephen T. *Alphabet City*. Viking, 1995. (Z shape in structure.)

Kalman, Maira. *What Pete Ate A–Z*. Putnam, 2001. ("Zug zug dog grub.")

Krull, Kathleen. *M Is for Music*. Illustrated by Stacy Innerst. Harcourt, 2003. (Zydeco, zither, zippy music.)

MacDonald, Ross. *Achoo! Bang! Crash! The Noisy Alphabet*. Roaring Brook, 2003. (Zip, zap, zig, zoom.)

The Metropolitan Museum of Art. *Museum ABC*. Little, Brown, 2002. (Zigzag.)

Milich, Zoran. *The City ABC Book*. Kids Can, 2001. (Z shape in a structure.)

Pelletier, David. *The Graphic Alphabet*. Orchard, 1996. (Zigzag.)

Polacco, Patricia. *G Is for Goat*. Philomel, 2003. (Z . . . amazing!)

Rogers, Jacqueline. *Kindergarten ABC*. Scholastic, 2002. (Zero, zoo, and look for the zebra, zebu, zeppelin, zinnia, and zipper.)

Shannon, George. *Tomorrow's Alphabet*. Illustrated by Donald Crews. Greenwillow, 1996. (Zero.)

CRAFT ACTIVITY

Making Zoo Flakes Based on the Book *Zoo Flakes ABC* by Will C. Howell

Howell, Will C. *Zoo Flakes ABC*. Walker, 2002.

Zoo flakes are snowflake-style paper cuts featuring a different animal for each letter of the alphabet. Provide paper and scissors. Directions for making your own zoo flake are given in the back of the book. This is a very unique craft activity for the kids to learn.

Mix and Match Picture Books

Adams, Georgie. *The Three Little Witches Storybook*. Illustrated by Emily Booth. Hyperion, 2002.

The youngest Harry Potter fans will enjoy these short stories of the witches Zara, Ziggy, and Zoe. Read either "Zoe's Tidy Spell," in which their magic goes wrong, or "Wizard Wink's School," in which the girls join their many classmates at a magical school that has a habit of changing its location from time to time.

Asch, Frank. *Ziggy Piggy and the Three Little Pigs*. Kids Can, 1998.

Meet Ziggy, the fourth little pig. Ziggy saves his three siblings when the Big Bad Wolf blows down the house made of straw, the house made of sticks, AND the house made of bricks. "This never happened before."

McDermott, Gerald. *Zomo the Rabbit: A Trickster Tale from West Africa*. Harcourt, 1992.

Clever Zomo asks the Sky God for wisdom, but in order to earn wisdom, Zomo is sent to do three impossible tasks. First, he must bring back the scales of Big Fish. Next, he must bring back the milk of Wild Cow. Finally, Zomo needs to return with a tooth of Leopard. The illustration of the naked Big Fish is hilarious.

Munsch, Robert. *Zoom!* Illustrated by Michael Martchenko. Scholastic, 2003.

Lauretta wants a new wheelchair but finds each one to be too slow. She finally gets a "nice new 92-speed, black, silver, and red, dirt-bike wheel-chair." The audience can help make the "ZOOOOOM" noises.

Steig, William. *Zeke Pippin*. HarperCollins, 1994.

Zeke finds a strange harmonica that causes all who listen to it to fall asleep. No matter how much Zeke "zeezled and zoozled," his family wouldn't stay awake. Zeke leaves home but runs into a gang of dogs and a "death-dealing coyote."

Tavares, Matt. *Zachary's Ball*. Candlewick, 2000.

Although this book comes across as an imitation of Van Allsburg's picture book *The Polar Express* in both art medium and story line, it is still a touching book. Zachary finds magic in a baseball that he catches in Fenway Park.

Viorst, Judith. *The Alphabet from Z to A (with Much Confusion on the Way)*. Illustrated by Richard Hull. Atheneum, 1994.

This rhyming alphabet narrative begins with the letter Z and goes backward. Viorst wonders why *xylophone* doesn't start with Z. She points out other "quirks and quagmires of the English language," such as *Y* is not for *using* and *X* is not for *excellent.*

Waber, Bernard. *The Mouse That Snored.* Houghton Mifflin, 2000.

A mouse disrupts a very quiet household with his very loud snores. The snores are so loud that the entire house shakes. Have the audience help produce a group snore to equal that of the little mouse.

Mix and Match Chapter Book Selections

Henkes, Kevin. *The Zebra Wall.* Greenwillow, 1988.

The Vorlob family has five girls named Adine, Bernice, Carla, Dot, and Effie. The whole family is so sure that the next child will also be a girl that they make a list of girl's names that begin with the letter *F.* Of course, they instead have a son. Read the first half of chapter 12. Mrs. Vorlob decides that her son—their last child—will have a name that begins with the letter *Z.* Finish the selection with Dot singing, "My brother's name is Zorro."

Lowry, Lois. *Zooman Sam.* Houghton Mifflin, 1999.

Preschooler Sam Krupnik (Anastasia's younger brother) is dressed as a zookeeper for Future Job Day. Read the second half of chapter 6, starting with the line, "Every single boy except Sam was a firefighter." Sam impatiently waits for the pouting Becky to explain her future job. It's a hilarious scene that will have the elementary-age crowd laughing.

Sadler, Marilyn. *Bobo Crazy.* Random House, 2001.

Introduce this series about a futuristic girl who lives in a space station by reading chapter 12, "Zenon's Guide to Space Station Slang." This glossary defines terms such as *Martian Mist,* "When your mind is kind of foggy and confused, you're in a Martian Mist," and *Z-Mart,* the space station's only discount store. Bobo is the robot dog that Zenon purchases at the local Z-Mart.

Scieszka, Jon. *It's All Greek to Me.* Viking, 1999.

The Time Warp Trio encounters Zeus and the other Greek gods. Set up the selection by telling your audience that the boys have a magic book that allows them to travel through time. They happened to be dressed in togas and carrying aluminum-foil-covered lightning bolts when they go back into the imaginary past. Read chapter 4. The three boys meet Zeus, who soon hides from Hera. Funny scenes include Sam trading insults with the mighty goddess.

Mix and Match Songs

Consider playing one of the following song titles that feature the letter Z in place of or in addition to Chapin's "Zag Zig."

> Greg and Steve. "Zip-a-Dee-Doo-Dah." In *Playing Favorites* (recording). Youngheart, 1991. This song can also be found on many Disney compilations.
>
> Paxton, Tom. "Goin' to the Zoo." In *Goin' to the Zoo* (recording). Rounder, 1997.
>
> Raffi. "Les Zombies et les Loups-Garous." In *The Corner Grocery Store* (recording). MCA, 1979.

Mix and Match Poetry

Florian, Douglas. "I Friz, I Froze." In *Bing Bang Boing*. Harcourt, 1994.

———. "The Zebras." In *Mammalabilia*. Harcourt, 2000.

———. "Zero Hero." In *Laugh-eteria*. Harcourt, 1999.

Lansky, Bruce. "Zachary Brown" and "Zoo Rules." In *If Pigs Could Fly and Other Deep Thoughts*. Illustrated by Stephen Carpenter. Meadowbrook, 2000.

Prelutsky, Jack. "Her Highness Zookeepoo." In *It's Raining Pigs and Noodles*. Illustrated by James Stevenson. Greenwillow, 2000.

———. "Zany Zapper Zockke" and "The Zoosher." In *The New Kid on the Block*. Illustrated by James Stevenson. Greenwillow, 1984.

———. "Zeke McPeake." In *A Pizza the Size of the Sun*. Illustrated by James Stevenson. Greenwillow, 1996.

———. "The Zoo Was in an Uproar." In *Something Big Has Been Here*. Illustrated by James Stevenson. Greenwillow, 1990.

Stevenson, James. "At the Zoo." In *Corn-Fed*. Greenwillow, 2002.

Wilbur, Richard. "Because They're Always BUZZING." In *The Disappearing Alphabet*. Illustrated by David Diaz. Harcourt, 1998.

Worth, Valerie. "Zinnias." In *All the Small Poems and Fourteen More.* Illustrated by Natalie Babbitt. Farrar, Straus and Giroux, 1994.

Tweaking the Program Theme . . .

. . . For Preschoolers

Drop the O'Malley and Waber picture books, the Singer short story selection, and the Van Allsburg picture book and dramatics, and substitute the following picture books:

Gay, Michel. *Zee.* Clarion, 2003.

> Zee, a tiny zebra, tries to wake up his sleepy parents by making them coffee. When he spills his tray, he pours what's left into teeny cups from the dolls' tea set.

Kvasnosky, Laura McGee. *Zelda and Ivy.* Candlewick, 1998.

> Read any or all of the three stories featuring two fox sisters. Zelda, the oldest, persuades Ivy to perform a "death-defying trick" on a playground swing in the first story. In the second story, Zelda decorates Ivy's tail, and in the last story, Zelda learns to share her new baton.

Paterson, Brian. *Zigby Hunts for Treasure: The Zebra Who Trots into Trouble.* HarperCollins, 2003.

> Zigby goes on a treasure hunt with Bertie Bird, an African guinea fowl, and McMeer, a meerkat.

Yaccarino, Dan. *Zoom! Zoom! Zoom! I'm Off to the Moon!* Scholastic, 1997.

> A young boy leaves home, puts on a space suit, straps inside a rocket, and blasts off into outer space and on to the moon and back.

. . . For Fifth and Sixth Graders

Drop the Bryan picture book, and replace it with the following oral story:

MacDonald, Margaret Read. "A Blind Man Catches a Bird." In *Peace Tales.* Linnet, 1992.

> A sighted man deceives his older, blind brother-in-law in this tale from Zimbabwe. The brother-in-law learns of the deception but teaches the younger man to not only correct this deception, but to become friends.

And Yet Even More Titles That Somehow Feature
the Letter Z for You to Consider

Aardema, Verna. *Bimwili and Zimwi: A Tale from Zanzibar.* Illustrated by Susan Meddaugh. Dial, 1985.

Bottner, Barbara. *Zoo Song.* Illustrated by Lynn Munsinger. Scholastic, 1987.

Dr. Seuss. *If I Ran the Zoo.* Random House, 1950.

Dr. Seuss. *On beyond Zebra.* Random House, 1955.

Ernst, Lisa Campbell. *Zinnia and Dot.* Viking, 1992.

Gershator, Phillis. *Zzzng! Zzzng! Zzzng! A Yoruba Tale.* Illustrated by Theresa Smith. Orchard, 1998.

Hru, Dakari. *The Magic Moonberry Jump Ropes.* Illustrated by E. B. Lewis. Dial, 1996. (Features Uncle Zambezi.)

Kimmel, Eric. The *Rooster's Antlers: A Story of the Chinese Zodiac.* Illustrated by YongSheng Xuan. Holiday House, 1999.

Lobel, Arnold. *A Zoo for Mister Muster.* HarperCollins, 1962.

McCully, Emily Arnold. *ZaZa's Big Break.* HarperCollins, 1989.

Miller, M. L. *The Enormous Snore.* Illustrated by Kevin Hawkes. Putnam, 1995.

Moss, Lloyd. *Zin! Zin! Zin! A Violin.* Illustrated by Marjorie Priceman. Simon and Schuster, 1995.

Munsch, Robert. *Fifty Below Zero.* Illustrated by Michael Martchenko. Annick, 1986.

Palatini, Margie. *Zoom Broom.* Illustrated by Howard Fine. Hyperion, 1998.

Peet, Bill. *Zella, Zack, and Zodiac.* Houghton Mifflin, 1986.

Pulver, Robin. *Mrs. Toggle's Zipper.* Illustrated by R. W. Alley. Four Winds, 1990.

Steig, William. *The Zabajaba Jungle.* Farrar, Straus and Giroux, 1987.

Stevenson, James. *Sam the Zamboni Man.* Greenwillow, 1998.

Van Allsburg, Chris. *The Wreck of the Zephyr.* Houghton Mifflin, 1983.

———. *Zathura.* Houghton Mifflin, 2002.

AUTHOR AND TITLE INDEX

Rob Reid is a lecturer for the Foundations of Education Department at the University of Wisconsin–Eau Claire. His specialty is children's literature, literature for adolescents, and storytelling. He is the author of three other ALA books, *Something Funny Happened at the Library* (2003), *Family Storytime* (1999), and *Children's Jukebox* (1995), as well as articles for *LibrarySparks* magazine and *School Library Journal*. He has previously served as a youth services and special needs consultant for the Indianhead Federated Library System in Eau Claire, Wisconsin, and as a children's librarian for the Eau Claire Public Library and the Pueblo (Colorado) Library District. He is an active member of the American Library Association, having served on the Great Websites Committee. He was elected to the 2006 Newbery Award Committee. Reid received his master's degree in library science from the University of Minnesota. In addition to teaching, Reid visits schools and libraries as a children's humorist and travels across the United States and Canada speaking to library and school organizations on story programming.